Cambridge Elements ≡

Elements in Experimental Political Science
edited by
James N. Druckman
Northwestern Universit

EXAMINING MOTIVATIONS IN INTERPERSONAL COMMUNICATION EXPERIMENTS

Elizabeth C. Connors
University of South Carolina

Matthew T. Pietryka
Florida State University

John Barry Ryan
Stony Brook University

CAMBRIDGE
UNIVERSITY PRESS

CAMBRIDGE
UNIVERSITY PRESS

University Printing House, Cambridge CB2 8BS, United Kingdom

One Liberty Plaza, 20th Floor, New York, NY 10006, USA

477 Williamstown Road, Port Melbourne, VIC 3207, Australia

314–321, 3rd Floor, Plot 3, Splendor Forum, Jasola District Centre, New Delhi – 110025, India

103 Penang Road, #05–06/07, Visioncrest Commercial, Singapore 238467

Cambridge University Press is part of the University of Cambridge.

It furthers the University's mission by disseminating knowledge in the pursuit of education, learning, and research at the highest international levels of excellence.

www.cambridge.org
Information on this title: www.cambridge.org/9781009114288
DOI: 10.1017/9781009110327

First published 2022

A catalogue record for this publication is available from the British Library.

ISBN 978-1-009-11428-8 Paperback
ISSN 2633-3368 (online)
ISSN 2633-335X (print)

Cambridge University Press has no responsibility for the persistence or accuracy of URLs for external or third-party internet websites referred to in this publication and does not guarantee that any content on such websites is, or will remain, accurate or appropriate.

Examining Motivations in Interpersonal Communication Experiments

Elements in Experimental Political Science

DOI: 10.1017/9781009110327
First published online: September 2022

Elizabeth C. Connors
University of South Carolina

Matthew T. Pietryka
Florida State University

John Barry Ryan
Stony Brook University

Author for correspondence: Elizabeth C. Connors,
ecconnors@gmail.com

Abstract: Does interpersonal political communication improve the quality of individual decision-making? While deliberative theorists offer reasons for hope, experimental researchers have demonstrated that biased messages can travel via interpersonal social networks. We argue that the value of interpersonal political communication depends on the motivations of the people involved, which can be shifted by different contexts. Using small-group experiments that randomly assign participants' motivations to seek or share information with others as well as their motivations for evaluating the information they receive, we demonstrate the importance of accounting for motivations in communication. We find that when individuals with more extreme preferences are motivated to acquire and share information, collective civic capacity is diminished. But if we can stimulate the exchange of information among individuals with stronger prosocial motivations, such communication can enhance collective civic capacity. We also provide advice for other researchers about conducting similar group-based experiments to study political communication.

Keywords: interpersonal communication, group experiments, motivations

JEL classifications: A12, B34, C56, D78, E90

The appendix for this Element can be found online at:
https://cambridge.org/examining-motivations-appendix

ISBNs: 9781009114288 (PB), 9781009110327 (OC)
ISSNs: 2633-3368 (online), 2633-335X (print)

Contents

1 Introduction

In *An Economic Theory of Democracy*, Anthony Downs (1957) proposes a solution to the problem of electorates who lack the interest, ability, or time to engage with politics. Essentially, he calls for a division of labor in which those who have the interest, ability, and time to engage with politics pay attention, and the rest of the public asks those people how they should vote and what their opinions on key issues should be. To avoid being misled, those who need this cheap information should seek out informants who have similar political preferences. Otherwise, the informant may advise them to support a candidate or policy that promotes the *informant*'s preferences while undermining the recipient's goals. This sender-receiver framework is a logical solution to the problem of poorly informed electorates that has spawned a long research agenda – including many experiments, some of which we conducted (e.g., Krupnikov et al., 2020; Pietryka, 2016; Ryan, 2011b).

But this framework is an odd description of human interactions. The oddity derives from the motivations of the actors in the model. First, the theoretical communication is instrumental, initiated by the person who lacks information. If this person does not seek advice, the interaction would never take place (at least as described by Downs [1957]). Yet people who lack political information often *avoid* – rather than seek – political discussions (Carlson & Settle, 2022), suggesting that this framework mischaracterizes the motivations driving such conversations.

Instead, these conversations are more likely to be initiated by informants, since they are the ones who are most interested in politics (Huckfeldt & Mendez, 2008). In fact, informed people – rather than the uninformed who, according to Downs, *should* be initiating communication – initiate political communication all the time. Krupnikov and Ryan (2022) demonstrate that those who are "deeply involved" in politics are those who are most likely to talk – and post on social media – about politics. They hold more extreme political preferences and tend to be more affectively polarized (see also Klar, Krupnikov, & Ryan, 2018).

This framework also assumes these conversations are motivated by political concerns – that is, it assumes people seek informants who are best able to provide them with political information. Individuals *could* select these informants from their broader social networks (see, e.g., Eveland & Kleinman, 2013), but this assumption conflicts with most observed political discussion networks. Instead of conducting a motivated search for political informants, people more commonly encounter political discussion as a byproduct of everyday conversations (Minozzi et al., 2020). As a result, the political informants people rely on most heavily are the same people they most frequently discuss other important matters with – often their close friends and family (Klofstad, McClurg, & Rolfe, 2009).

Further, in the basic Downsian model, the only way people can trust an informant is when they have shared political preferences. This is primarily because it is assumed that the informant's main goal is persuading others to reach the same conclusions they have reached when two people with conflicting preferences should reach different conclusions. Certainly, individuals send biased messages about politics – this tendency is reflected in the importance of discussion network partisanship in voting decisions (Ryan, 2010; Sokhey & McClurg, 2012) – but it is unlikely that the Downsian model characterizes most political discussion: if it did, preferences would merge enough that disagreement in networks could not survive (Huckfeldt, Mendez, & Osborn, 2004). Instead, people often discuss politics for reasons *other* than information seeking or persuasion (Lyons & Sokhey, 2014): people often discuss politics to maintain social bonds, exchange perspectives, or just pass time (Carlson & Settle, 2022; Conover, Searing, & Crewe, 2002; Eveland, Morey, & Hutchens, 2011). Yet, in Downs's framework, informants gain no satisfaction from such social motivations.

In sum, Downs envisions a world in which political discussion occurs because individuals who lack sufficient political information seek more-expert informants. And these informants care more about furthering their political goals than helping others, sharing their expertise, or maintaining healthy relationships. These exchanges do not seem to offer a "solution" to the problem of electorates who lack the interest, ability, or time to engage with politics. Nor do they seem to reflect what discussion actually looks like, where communication is often intended to fulfill motivations *beyond* political information seeking and is associated with a general interest in politics on the part of the person doing the talking.

And yet the experimental research on interpersonal communication supports Downs (1957). Participants tend to prefer more expert sources (Ahn & Ryan, 2015; Pietryka, 2016). They send biased summaries of the news (Carlson, 2019). They make worse decisions when receiving information from people with different preferences (Krupnikov et al., 2020; Lupia & McCubbins, 1998; Ryan, 2011b). In all, much of the experimental literature suggests interpersonal communication is indeed driven by partisan motivations (Ahn, Huckfeldt, & Ryan, 2014) with little aggregate enlightenment as a result (Jackman & Sniderman, 2006).

One critique of this experimental literature – and a potential explanation for findings that support Downs (1957) despite his odd assumptions – is that the results in these previous experiments are only externally valid to contexts in which participants have motivations similar to the ones that Downs (1957) was talking about. A related critique is that the experimental designs either explicitly or implicitly motivate participants to think like Downs would expect them to. The experiments are often explicitly built around a model in which communication arises from information seeking rather than to fulfill other motivations. The researchers do not tell participants that trust only comes from shared political preferences, but since the instructions explicitly frame the experiments in political terms and emphasize preferences, they imply that preferences are a key element. It thus should be no surprise that participants' behavior is driven by these preferences (see Groenendyk & Krupnikov, 2021).

If we are going to build a model that extends to more common interpersonal discussion contexts than the one put forth by Downs and subsequent experiments, we need to do so explicitly. Thus, in this Element, we primarily discuss experiments in the behavioral economics tradition, incentivizing participants to consider motivations besides the ones typical in the Downsian perspective. After explaining our experimental framework in Section 2, we move beyond the information-seeking model of interpersonal communication (Section 3). There are incentives for participants to seek information, but also to *send* information. Further, we include treatments in which the motivation to acquire information from news sources is correlated with the desire to send messages – as Krupnikov and Ryan (2022) would suggest is fairly common. In Section 4, we introduce the possibility that individuals might have prosocial motivations in addition to their partisan and accuracy ones. That is, we create incentives to help others in the experiment, just as real-world informants are often motivated to help their friends and family.

The results suggest that motivations matter. When participants have incentives that align with Downs's model, interpersonal communication promotes the welfare of experts at the expense of the less informed. For instance, when the most interested also tend to have the most extreme preferences, moderates tend to be poorly represented (Section 3). On the other hand, the introduction of prosocial motivations in Section 4 shows greater potential for individuals to improve their political decisions via communication. Together, the results suggest that interpersonal communication is most likely to be effective as a political information shortcut when the motivations behind the communication are not political – especially when individuals receive less of a benefit from persuading others. This finding, especially when combined with the accumulated literature (see Krupnikov & Ryan, 2022; Minozzi et al., 2020; Settle, 2018), gives greater hope to the value of interpersonal discussion for collective civic capacity than discussion via social media.

The designs of our experiments are built off the basic design in other interpersonal communication experiments in the behavioral economics tradition (e.g., Ahn et al., 2014; Krupnikov et al., 2020; Pietryka, 2016) and are expanded upon in more detail in Section 2. In these studies, participants are brought into a laboratory in groups to participate in a mock election. Researchers can vary features of the election, such as the candidates' policy positions, the participants' policy positions, and how participants learn about these positions. Importantly, researchers provide incentives to the participants that determine what motivates participant behavior – whether the researchers know this is what they are doing or not (see Groenendyk & Krupnikov, 2021).

We provide an outline of the experiments in Figure 1 – we build on and edit this figure in our experimental descriptions in Sections 3 and 4. At the first stage in each election, the experimental factors are randomly assigned, as are the positions of two computer-generated candidates and the positions of each participant. In our experiments, these factors are designed to incentivize specific motivations – we discuss this after explaining how participants learn about the candidates. In each election, participants are voters who are each assigned an integer position on a numeric scale with no defined policy content. The participants must choose between two "candidates" who are not fellow participants but whose numbers represent the candidates' positions on the aforementioned scale. Participants gain money when the candidate closest to their position wins

Stage 1. The election begins

  Experimental factors assigned

  Candidates' positions assiged

  Participants' positions assigned

Stage 2. Private information and first judgment

  Participants view private information

  Each signal drawn randomly from uniform distribution centered on candidate's true position ± 3

  After viewing information, participants enter estimates of each candidate's position

Stage 3. Social information and second judgment

  Participants choose with whom to communicate

  Participants send information

  Participants enter updated estimates of the candidates' positions

Stage 4. Vote

  Participants vote

Stage 5. Outcome

  Participants learn winner of election and the rewards they received

  The winner of the election determined by majority rule

A new election begins at Stage 1

Figure 1 An overview of the stages in an election experiment

the election. The candidates' positions are unknown to participants, but they can learn about these positions in two ways: private information and social information.

In Stage 2 of each election, participants can obtain **private information** that is noisy but unbiased on average, mimicking the acquisition of impersonal sources like news media. Like in the real world, participants' expertise varies – in the experiments, expertise is measured as the amount of private information the participant has received. After obtaining the private information, in Stage 3, participants can also obtain **social information** from fellow participants, mimicking interpersonal communication. Regardless of whether the information is private or social, each piece of information contains two integer signals indicating estimates of each candidate's position.

Subjects make three judgments. The first is an estimate of the candidates' positions after receiving private information (Stage 2). The second is a (potentially) updated estimate of the candidates' positions after receiving the social information (Stage 3). These two judgments allow us to see how interpersonal communication affects participants' beliefs about the candidates. The final judgment comes in Stage 4 when participants vote for a candidate. This is the most consequential judgment since it determines the payoffs of the election – though the exact incentives vary in each experiment, participants always receive more money when the victor is the closest candidate to their position. This winner is revealed in Stage 5, after which a new election begins at Stage 1.

Our key experimental factors are designed to manipulate motivations by randomly assigning payoffs that are not exclusively based on the election outcome. In the experiments featured in Section 3, subjects receive (or lose) money based on whether they participate in the interpersonal communication stage. The actual discussion payoff is randomly assigned at the individual level. At the group level, we randomly assign the correlations between the participants' discussion payoffs, positions, and expertise.

In Section 4, we incentivize prosocial considerations by paying some participants based on the decision of their discussion partners – that is, the senders are paid if the receivers "vote correctly" (Lau & Redlawsk, 1997). On one hand, this incentivizes senders to truthfully reveal to receivers how they believe the receivers should vote. On the other hand, if the senders and receivers have different preferred candidates, then the senders lower their probability of receiving the election payoff if they earn the prosocial payoff. Hence, it is not a forgone conclusion that subjects will be helpful in the prosocial treatment.

We obviously value the findings in previous experimental studies, but the new experiments discussed in this Element are important additions to the literature since nonpartisan motivations affect every stage of interpersonal political communication, from the decision to join a conversation to how people react after a conversation has ended. This point is a core contribution of Carlson and Settle (2022). We hope their work shifts attention to the importance of motivations, but more work is needed: since their impressive designs do not randomly assign motivations, they lack the ability to identify the effects of motivations or distinguish between the effects of different motivations (Leeper & Slothuus, 2014).

This is why we advocate for studying interpersonal communication motivations in laboratory settings as we have done here. Of course, the experiments described here are abstract, which limits their external validity. Further, the motivations we examine are not an exhaustive list of all motivations that may be relevant for interpersonal political communication – nor do they include all the motivations that can be experimentally manipulated. We therefore conclude this Element with a discussion of both the promise and perils of studying motivations in interpersonal communication via laboratory experiments.

2 Our Experimental Framework

Social influence, including interpersonal communication, is not an understudied aspect of society and there has been wide variation in approaches to its study. Some researchers have approached it from a purely theoretical perspective (e.g., Calvert, 1985; Crawford & Sobel, 1982), including some that expanded the theoretical analysis to include numerous actors (e.g., Rolfe, 2012; Siegel, 2009). Others built on these theoretical models to run experiments (e.g., Carlson, 2019) occasionally with "real stakes" (e.g., Ahn et al., 2014; Krupnikov et al., 2020; Lupia & McCubbins, 1998). Obviously, researchers have used the workhorse of public opinion studies, the survey, to examine social influence (e.g., Huckfeldt & Sprague, 1995; Mutz, 2006; Sokhey & McClurg, 2012). Increased computing power has allowed for the expanded study of social influence with actors embedded inside larger social networks (e.g., Lazer et al., 2010; Song & Eveland, 2015).

Regardless of approach, the fundamental building block of all of these studies is a dyadic interaction that takes on a similar form. An individual (the sender) provides information to another individual (the receiver). These interactions are at the heart of even the fanciest agent-based model or social-network analysis. The analyses that expand beyond the two actors are simply studying the dynamic consequences of *many* of these dyadic interactions happening at once or over time.

Experiments are particularly well suited for this type of study because observational studies are plagued by endogeneity issues that are difficult to resolve (Fowler et al., 2011; Huckfeldt, 2007; Huckfeldt & Mendez, 2008) and because they also lack important information necessary to demonstrate actual social influence. For example, there is some level of individual choice in social influence. Many people actively seek out information via both the news media and their friends – further, they choose to accept or reject the information they receive (Zaller, 1992). On the other hand, individuals do not have *full* control over the flow of information and thus over social influence. In the modern world, the acquisition of information has the feeling of drinking from a fire hose. Messages can essentially sneak in, producing important consequences for citizens' informational biases (Huckfeldt, 1983; Huckfeldt & Sprague, 1995). While most surveys will miss these nuances (see Carlson & Settle, 2022), even in the most thorough survey, neither these messages nor their source will be reported due to respondents' lack of awareness they are receiving them.

Carefully designed laboratory experiments can address these obstacles, allowing for analysis at the dyadic level that can form the basis of the study of more complex processes. As we discussed in Section 1, the experimental frameworks we rely on in this Element are incentivized studies based on a Downsian (Downs, 1957) spatial model of political preference and competition. And as we have noted in *this* section, there are many other approaches – including experimental approaches – to addressing questions related to social influence. At the same time, we see several advantages to utilizing a spatial model. First, these designs allow us to easily assign all potential senders, receivers, and candidates a position on a single dimension. Hence, it becomes possible to talk about the "distance" between any pair of citizens or candidates on a continuum – that is, preferences.

Second, we can more easily incorporate concepts of interest that are difficult or impossible to randomly assign in an experiment (let alone to examine in an observational setting). For example, our interest in political expertise in Section 3 necessitates random assignment of political expertise. The Downsian framework allows us to do this: we can examine political expertise by incorporating political uncertainty. Of course, political expertise presupposes uncertainty – if everyone has perfect information about politics, then everyone will be equally expert at politics, making the concept of expertise irrelevant.

Indeed, spatial models of political competition abound in which citizens are more or less informed about the candidates' true positions or the ultimate impact of a proposed policy on the citizen's own welfare (e.g., Baron, 1994; Budge, 1994; Calvert, 1985; Shepsle, 1972). Level of expertise can be represented in various ways, including the proximity of a voter's estimate of a candidate's true position to the actual policy position of the candidate, the variability of a voter's estimate of a candidate's position, or the amount of information a voter has acquired. In this way, we can incorporate not only the heterogeneity in preferences but also variation in expertise.

These advantages are well understood and well studied. One potential issue is that they may also be well understood by experimental *participants*. As discussed in Section 1, the way researchers communicate experiments to participants can lead participants to behave in particular ways (Groenendyk & Krupnikov, 2021). As a result, when a design focuses on preferences and expertise – and, therefore, experimental instructions explicitly mention preferences and expertise – participants might believe that they should primarily consider preferences and expertise in their decision-making within the experiment. Participants concentrating on preferences is especially concerning given that effective interpersonal communication is difficult because of the frequency with which people send biased information (e.g., Carlson, 2019; Ryan, 2011b). Leading participants to prioritize preferences might exacerbate this, which might suggest that interpersonal communication is hopelessly plagued by motivated reasoning and self-interest – *or* it might be that participants act self-interested because they believe that is what the researchers want them to do.

The good news is we can amend traditional group-based, incentivized experimental designs to take into account other potential motivations in political discussion *beyond* the simple partisan motivations of the sender. Doing so is crucial because observational work suggests the effects of interpersonal communication are strongly correlated with participants' motivations (Eveland, 2004). One advantage of previous experiments is that expertise is manipulated by presenting participants with a set of information that is unbiased – this avoids inferential problems caused by partisan differences in information the subject brings to the experiment (Tappin, Pennycook, & Rand, 2020) and allows for clear identification of behavior consistent with partisan motivations. The weakness, however, is that researchers cannot test what consequences result when partisan motivations are mixed with *other* motivations.

Despite the plethora of studies looking at interpersonal communication, one would be hard-pressed to write a literature review of experiments examining how different motivations affect social influence. An exception is Pietryka's (2016) study, which explicitly introduces accuracy motivations to the design – demonstrating that people do not necessarily make more accurate decisions when they are motivated to do so. This finding also demonstrates a broader implication for the study of motivations: if accuracy motivations do not necessarily increase accuracy, the *effects* of motivations may differ from their *intent*. Thus, since these effects cannot be inferred, we can better understand them through experiments that randomly assign different motivations.

The experimental innovations we discuss are similar to Pietryka's as we also randomly assign nonpartisan motivations to participants. Random assignment to motivations is the only way to know that the outcomes we observe are the result of differences in motivations and not some other process we failed to consider (Leeper & Slothuus, 2014). By the end of this Element, we will demonstrate that these types of design choices have implications for our understanding of the effects of interpersonal communication. Introducing other motivations can either amplify or attenuate the bias in both the messages people send and the perceptions of the messages people receive, ultimately shaping how democracy functions. Hence, the efficacy of a discussion depends on which motivations shape that discussion.

2.1 Current Approaches and Findings

At the most basic level, researchers conduct interpersonal communication experiments in the hopes of understanding what will happen in versions of the following hypothetical scenario: someone, who we will call Rob, is deciding between two or more options and someone else, who we will call Samara, provides him with some information about the options. Researchers build their treatments around this basic scenario. For example, the information Samara provides Rob may not be accurate either due to Samara's ignorance or deliberate dissembling. Or, Rob may not need Samara's information – Rob may actually already have enough information to make the decision that is best for his interests. Experimenters might *also* vary whether or not Rob specifically requested information from Samara or if Samara was assigned to send information to Rob.

Another key factor in almost all of these experiments is whether Samara and Rob have preferences that are aligned – recall from Section 1 this is important in the Downsian framework. That is, an important experimental treatment is whether Samara is better off if Rob makes the right choice for Rob (i.e., their preferences are aligned) or if Samara is *worse* off if Rob makes the right choice for Rob (i.e., their preferences are at odds). This could be manipulated in several ways. For example, the experimenter could create political parties (as in Ryan, 2011b) and Rob and Samara could be in the same party or different parties. Alternatively, the experimenter could place Samara and Rob on an abstract policy dimension and vary how close Samara's and Rob's positions are on that scale (as in Ahn, Huckfeldt, & Ryan, 2010).

The logic of what will occur in interactions of this type is laid out in Downs (1957) as well as Crawford and Sobel (1982), and expanded upon by Calvert (1985) and Lupia and McCubbins (1998). If Rob's (i.e., the receiver's) preferences are aligned with Samara's (i.e., the sender's) preferences, then Samara will send a signal Samara believes to be accurate. If Rob and Samara have divergent preferences, then Samara may send a self-serving signal if she can get away with it (e.g., if Samara does not care that her deception might hurt her relationship with Rob or if Samara believes Rob will never find out the truth).

If the signal is clearly self-serving, then Rob should ignore it. The consequence of this dynamic is that interpersonal communication is not beneficial in many situations. For example, imagine Rob is a Democrat trying to decide how to vote in a local election. If Samara is a Democrat, then Samara will likely tell Rob to vote Democratic – this is probably what Rob was going to do without any information from Samara. If Samara is a Republican, then maybe Samara will try to convince Rob to go against his party, but Rob should ignore that information. Rob can only benefit from Samara's signal if Samara is a Democrat who says, "In this election, our party's candidate is so bad that you should vote Republican."

This is because partisanship provides Rob with free information. Rob will also have free information if he has a position on a policy scale and knows that a particular type of candidate tends to be on the same side of the policy scale. Hence, Lupia and McCubbins (1998) point out that in many situations interpersonal communication can only harm decision makers who have some information that is pointing them in the right direction. More recent work finds communication to be particularly harmful for women, who put more stock in social signals than men do and thus are led astray in most conditions (Krupnikov et al., 2020).[1] Last, Calvert (1985) observes that a receiver without a priori information can benefit from communication, but only if the communication does not clearly benefit the sender.

Given this, it is no surprise that in Ryan (2011b), participants who are assigned to a "party" (i.e., participants who have a candidate they should

---

[1] Krupnikov and colleagues (2020) also find that men ignore social signals too readily, including in the situation where the sender and receiver have aligned preferences and the signal is akin to "In this election, our party's candidate is so bad that you should vote for the other one."

support) are not more likely, after social communication, to choose the candidate who will offer them a greater payoff. Further, in some instances, "partisans" are worse off because they do not reject clearly self-serving signals. Only participants who are *not* assigned to a party benefit from communication because (1) senders do not always send self-serving signals and (2) when they do send self-serving signals, some of those signals happen to give independents useful information.

In Ahn and colleagues' (2014) book, which examines the results of a series of experiments, the authors conclude that "opinion leaders are not the reference librarians of democratic politics," explaining that "opinion leaders tend to be both experts and activists" – the point being that knowledgeable individuals, rather than simply inform, send signals with the hope of persuading individuals to choose their favored candidate or policy. On occasion, this will mean trying to convince someone to make a decision that goes against their preferences (i.e., sometimes Samara needs to mislead Rob to get Rob to vote the way Samara wishes).

In the Ahn and colleagues (2014) experiments, there are times when the sender knows they are clearly sending a misleading signal. In most of the experiments, participants are assigned positions on an abstract seven-point scale. They are choosing between two candidates, named A and B, who also have a position on that scale. Candidate A tends to have a position that is closer to 1 while Candidate B tends to have a position that is closer to 7, but their exact positions are unknown. In the experiments, it was never going to be the case that a subject assigned to a position at one extreme end of the scale will have the same preferred candidate as a subject assigned to the other extreme end of the scale.[2] Hence, senders at position 7 know they are lying if they send signals suggesting that receivers at position 1 should support the same candidate they do.

As noted in Section 1, in these experiments, the signals participants send to each other are estimates of the candidates' true positions based on noisy (but unbiased) private information that the experimenters assigned to participants. There are advantages to the signals being abstract like this. Most obviously, it is easy to quantify how accurately the sender's signal reflects the sender's true beliefs. It also maps onto typical ways in which people will mislead others about a candidate – they can make the candidate seem more or less extreme than they really are (Ahn & Ryan, 2015).

---

[2] If the candidates have the same position, then all participants are indifferent between the candidates. This is the closest the polar ends of the scale come to having similar preferences.

The downside is that the abstract nature of the signals mean that the sender cannot send biased signals without lying. In the world outside the laboratory, this is not the case. For example, imagine a Democratic candidate has five policies – two of which are fairly moderate and three of which are very extreme. A Democratic voter could try and persuade others to support this candidate by emphasizing the moderate policies and ignoring the extreme ones. This is very misleading about the candidate's true positions, but it is also not necessarily lying.

Carlson's (2018, 2019) experiments avoid many such threats to mundane realism evident in experiments in the experimental economics tradition. Participants are randomly assigned either to read a news article about the economy or to receive social messages about the article from participants who had read it. Carlson's results lead to similar conclusions as the more abstract incentivized experiments – which aligns with Brutger and colleagues (2020), who find that many experimental results replicate across both abstract and more concrete experimental setups. In Carlson's experiments, participants who received the social message learned less than the participants who read the article. Further, the participants in the social message treatment changed their evaluations of the economy and the president based on the partisanship of the subject who sent the message. This suggests the signals sent were biased in the direction of the sender's partisanship as in the previous experiments.

In sum, the existing experimental evidence calls into question the ability of interpersonal communication to lead to a more enlightened environment. Too many individuals have as their main goal seeing their preferences replicated among other participants for people to benefit from communication. This does not mean that people *never* benefit from communication, but it does seem that the best-case scenario is that communication helps some people and harms others. As a result, interpersonal communication has no beneficial effects in the aggregate (see also Jackman & Sniderman, 2006).

2.2 Instructing Participants

Carlson's (2019) experiments were carefully designed to capture how information goes from the news media to individuals who do not pay attention to the news. It is important to note, however, that the experiment's instructions may have elevated the importance of partisan considerations. When participants are writing their social messages, they are given the following instructions: "Imagine that you were discussing politics and current events with a [Republican/Democrat/Independent]. Please write what you would tell a [Republican/Democrat/Independent] about the article you just read." As in the more abstract experiments, the instructions direct a sender's attention to the political preferences of the receiver. This design choice makes sense because people typically have some sense of the partisanship of the people with whom they are speaking (Huckfeldt et al., 1999). On the other hand, it implies that participants should consider partisanship when sending the social message – when people participate in an experiment or a survey, they figure that the researcher is mentioning a particular piece of information because it is relevant (Klar et al., 2018).

As a result, the instructions participants receive can imply a motivation for responding to the stimuli (Connors, Krupnikov, & Ryan, 2019) – even when that was not the experimenter's intention. Indeed, Groenendyk and Krupnikov (2021) demonstrate that participants engage in partisan-motivated reasoning in political studies because they are told the study is about politics. Since the conventional wisdom is that politics is primarily about the conflict between two parties, they view the treatments they receive as a strong partisan would – even if that is not how they would process information in a typical situation.

In the case of the experimental literature examining the efficacy of interpersonal communication, there is an implicit instruction to prioritize partisan motivations. This is a problem for several reasons. The most obvious is that it could overstate the frequency with which people hold partisan motivations – participants behave like hard partisans whose primary goal is persuasion because the experiment emphasized that motivation above all others. Second, persuasion is just one of the many reasons people might participate in political discussion. For example, people may participate in political discussion simply because that is what is happening around them – that "participation" might even take the form of a pure listener who rarely contributes (Carlson & Settle, 2022).

Finally, the implicit nature of the motivations is a problem because not everyone will pick up on the implicit motivations. As a result, a confound is introduced if recognition of these motivations is correlated with some underlying variable. For example, a person who wants to cooperate might lie to other participants because they want to comply with what they believe the experimenter wants them to do. Outside the laboratory, this person might instead be *less* likely to lie because they would want to make the person they are talking to happy.

In this Element, we handle the issue of implicit motivations in a straightforward way: we make the motivations explicit. We directly incentivize participants to consider particular motivations when they participate in experiments. The underlying question is whether altering participants' motivations changes the conclusions from past research.

As we previously noted, directly incentivizing motivations has been rarely done in interpersonal communications experiments. The exception, Pietryka (2016), randomly assigns motivations to participants while keeping the framework of the experiments in Ahn and colleagues (2014).[3] In addition to the standard election payoff, some participants are randomly assigned to also receive a payment if they correctly guess unknown positions of the candidates. As a result, the participants are encouraged to engage in accuracy motivations – the other motivation commonly studied in political science besides partisan motivations (see, e.g., Bayes et al., 2020).

Did this change in motivations lead to more accurate estimates following social information? It did not. This does not mean, however, that participants did not change their behavior. Participants were allowed to choose who sent them social information, and those in the accuracy treatment sought out information from senders with a greater diversity of positions on the abstract scale. Part of the problem is that the participants chose senders with more information even if those senders had an incentive to send them biased information. And some of those participants sent self-serving signals, leading to a diminished capacity for them to make accurate estimates. The standard instructions cause individuals to attune to preferences and partisanship while these instructions cause participants to overvalue expertise (see also Ahn & Ryan, 2015).

Like the experiments that came before it, Pietryka's (2016) fails to demonstrate the means by which interpersonal communication leads to collective enlightenment, but it *does* point to the importance of motivations because participants did indeed change their behavior in response to the incentivized motivation. Thus, like Pietryka (2016), we take the basic experimental framework in Ahn and colleagues (2014) and introduce treatments that explicitly incentivize different motivations.[4] We need to explicitly incentivize motivations because one cannot infer them based on outcomes. We can see this from Pietryka's (2016) experiments – participants were clearly *motivated* to reach accurate conclusions yet failed to do so. Thus, as noted previously, random assignment to motivations is necessary.

---

[3] Another potential exception is Barabas (2004). He does not directly manipulate subject motivations, but, in the case of a deliberative forum, the discussion leader invokes the goal of keeping an open mind "early and often" (691). Barabas argues open-mindedness is an important prerequisite to successful deliberation.

[4] We do make additional changes to the design. For example, in Ahn and colleagues' (2014) experiments, participants typically participated in groups of seven and never more than fourteen. In the experiment covered in Section 3, participants participate in groups of twenty-five. But the broad design items (e.g., the candidates and voters on a single abstract dimension and the way communication occurs) is consistent with the previous work.

2.3 Incentivizing Motivations

Studying motivations in interpersonal communication is challenging because motivations are often fleeting. Therefore, they are difficult to observe for any individual participant in the discussion, let alone all participants. This observational challenge is only amplified in survey research – the dominant mode for the study of political attitudes and behavior (Robison et al., 2018) – since surveys are often fielded days, weeks, and sometimes months after the relevant discussions have ended. Further, these motivations are often correlated with other psychological dispositions, such as partisanship and interest, that are difficult to disentangle from one another.

To overcome these observational challenges, Leeper and Slothuus (2014) advocate for the study of motivated reasoning – that is, the motivation to reach certain conclusions when processing information – with experimental designs that exogenously shift these motivations. This is precisely what Groenendyk and Krupnikov (2021) do in their study: participants are given the same materials as in Taber and Lodge's (2006) seminal study of motivated reasoning, but Groenendyk and Krupnikov *also* randomly assign participants to different instructions – essentially randomly assigning partisan or nonpartisan motivations.

In both experiments, participants were told to evaluate the strength of different arguments regardless of their opinion about the issue under consideration. Taber and Lodge (2006) attempted to motivate an evenhanded evaluation of the arguments by telling participants they would receive information with which they might disagree, but they would have to "explain the debate." As Druckman (2012) notes, "Individuals may have understood this to mean that they need to present some facts to others, but not necessarily to justify their opinions; they may not have been induced to consider alternative considerations or the process by which they formed their opinions" (203). If Druckman is right, when participants were told they might disagree with some of the statements, they were also motivated to engage in partisan-motivated reasoning, even though this was not the researchers' intent.

The Groenendyk and Krupnikov (2021) experiments suggest this is exactly what happened. Participants were told they would receive "additional information," "political information," or information with which they "might disagree." They were then more likely to rate arguments they agreed with as strong in the "political information" and "might disagree" treatments than in the "additional information" treatment. Hence, one approach to examining motivations is altering the instructions the researcher gives to participants.

Unlike Groenendyk and Krupnikov's (2021) experiments, the experiments examined in this Element are in the experimental economics tradition, in which the treatments involve randomization of financial incentives. As in Ahn and colleagues (2014), the experiments are group-based and involve a simulated election. The key to incentivizing motivations beyond partisan motivations is to award payoffs for things that have nothing to do with the outcome of the simulated election.

To understand why we focus not just on electoral outcomes but also on the process of becoming informed, consider the following hypothetical. Imagine your incumbent member of Congress is a member of your party and also a horrible human being – they are corrupt, lying, and manipulative, and they hate puppies and kittens. One individual might process information about this incumbent with the desire to correctly judge how bad or good their member is – this desire exemplifies an accuracy motivation. Before deciding whether they will support the incumbent for reelection, this accuracy-motivated individual would seek a broad pool of information, giving each story careful scrutiny. Another individual might search for reasons to dismiss the negative information because they desire their party's candidates to be the best representative – this desire exemplifies a partisan motivation. Compared to the accuracy-motivated person, this partisan-motivated individual might spend less time seeking information and expend less effort processing the information they happen to stumble across. Ultimately, however, both of these hypothetical characters will typically vote for the party member; while this member is clearly terrible, their election makes control of the chamber more likely, something that both accuracy- and partisan-motivated individuals might want. Thus, if we just look at vote choice, it might appear that everyone is engaging in *partisan*-motivated reasoning, even though – if we were to look at how they were processing information – this is not the case.

Hence, we need to incentivize these other concerns and randomly assign these incentives to examine if certain motivations are having causal effects and, if so, what those effects are. There are myriad different motivations that we could look at, but we look at motivations that are directly tied to the process of interpersonal communication. We do so because the literature we are speaking to and the experimental designs on which we are basing our designs are experiments in interpersonal communication. We also do so because we, like Carlson and Settle (2022), believe there are motivations in political discussions that we do not fully understand the consequences of.

In Section 3, we are going to look at the motivation to acquire and share information. In some other experiments, certain participants must send signals – but often people want to engage in discussion only as listeners while others want to opt out of discussion entirely (Carlson & Settle, 2022). And of course, there are some people who are fans of talking about politics the way others are fans of talking about sports or movies. This desire is often associated with extremity or strong partisanship (Krupnikov & Ryan, 2022). For this reason, in Section 3, we will randomly assign whether the motivation to acquire and share information is correlated with extremity. This allows us to examine the consequences of this association.

Afterward, in Section 4, we will directly address partisan motivations and experimentally manipulate the importance of those motivations versus other motivations. In this experiment, stronger partisan motivations are encouraged by linking participants' incentives to the performance of a particular candidate. However, we can also induce stronger *accuracy* motivations by linking participants' incentives to the accuracy of their judgments about the candidates in the simulated elections – as Pietryka (2016) did.

We will go further, however, and introduce explicit incentives to combat the partisan motivations typical in these studies. Experiments in the tradition of behavioral economics are largely based around conflict (Del Ponte, Kline & Ryan, 2020). That participants with different preferences are in conflict is an implicit assumption in many of these experiments in the same way that self interest is an assumption in the base models many of these experiments are testing. Self-interest is an implicit assumption that can be relaxed, however, allowing for a model that considers that some participants will consider the payoffs of others (see, e.g., Fehr & Schmidt, 1999). Thus, in the experiment in Section 4, we will explicitly incentivize *prosocial* motivations by linking participants' incentives to the decisions of fellow participants.

In these experiments, we randomly assign treatments at both the group and individual levels. In Section 3, most of the treatments are assigned to groups, while in Section 4, all of the treatments are assigned to individuals. This helps broaden the opportunities for researchers – some research questions may require a group-level treatment, while others may require an individual-level treatment. Our Element demonstrates that both are possible. We return to this in more detail in the final section (Section 5).

Of course, our designs remove many important features of real-world political discussion and electoral politics. Perhaps most importantly, our design in Section 3 removes party labels from the participants' calculus, which thereby inhibits our ability to understand how partisanship might contribute to experts' motivations to acquire and share information. Yet this choice allows us to demonstrate that partisanship is not necessary to produce a system dominated by ideological extremists.

We have also previously mentioned another limitation of our approach: there is no role for rhetoric in these communications – there is no embellishment or shading of the truth. Participants can only lie, which (as we have noted) has the benefit of allowing us to quantify exactly how large their lies are. There is also no role for emotional language. This could be an issue, as people attune more to individual stories than to abstract figures (Krupnikov & Levine, 2019) and the messages in our experiments are only numbers. Theoretically, this could mean that the messages are less persuasive than those with more rhetorical flourishes. However, as we have previously noted, experiments such as these often find similar results to observational studies using survey data – for example, Ryan (2011b) and Sokhey and McClurg (2012) reach similar conclusions to Lau and Redlawsk (1997) about interpersonal communication and "correct voting." This suggests that the abstract communication in the laboratory replicates the important elements of communication outside of it, which, again, aligns with research replicating findings across abstract and concrete approaches to experiments (Brutger et al., 2020).

It should be clear that the goal of these experiments is not to replicate real elections nor is it to determine the frequency with which these different motivations exist in the population. Nor is our goal to pit the behaviors of our participants against some model of rational behavior – though obviously there is an underlying formal model that could be constructed for the dyadic interactions.

Rather, much like Ahn and colleagues (2014), we view these experiments as "exploratory," testing the consequences of situations that cannot be examined with standard data (Smith, 1982). For example, Krupnikov and Ryan (2022) argue that "deep involvement" (i.e., outsized engagement) in politics is inextricably linked to extremity and polarization. As a result, observational studies would struggle to separate out the effects of a strong motivation to acquire information and polarized attitudes. In our elections in Section 3, we can ensure those characteristics are orthogonal to each other or, alternatively, even more correlated than in the world outside the laboratory. The experimental treatments allow us to look at the direct effects of motivations in ways that simply are not possible via any other method. We turn next to this very experiment.

3 Motivating Information Seeking and Sharing

In this section, we present our first experiment, which examines how motivations of political extremists – or those with extreme preferences – can influence others as well as the collective.[5] We first note that political extremists are also often political experts (i.e., those in social networks who know more about politics than their peers) who have the motivation to acquire political information. We next note that, given their extreme preferences, extremists likely have the motivation to disseminate potentially biased information – *and*, because of their expertise, have the power to do so, influencing others in their networks who rely on them for information. Using our experimental setup described in Sections 1 and 2, we next test the outcomes of political extremists' motivations to acquire and share political information – randomly assigning these two motivations to those with extreme or not extreme preferences.

3.1 Background

Political expertise is not equally distributed among the public. Many Americans are woefully underinformed about politics (Delli Carpini & Keeter, 1996), lacking a coherent belief system and seemingly making political choices quite randomly (Converse, 1964). This revelation has disturbed political scientists for decades, leading them to wonder just how our democracy functions. One solution could lie in the power of social networks: the underinformed and under-interested can rely on political experts (i.e., ordinary people who pay an outsized level of attention to and are more informed about politics) in their social networks as informants (Carlson, 2019; McClurg, 2006).[6] In other words, without watching or reading the news, people can become relatively informed just by speaking with friends, family members, neighbors, and coworkers who are better politically informed than they are. This was the proposition from Downs (1957) discussed in Section 1.

Indeed, research finds that many people rely on their more expert associates for political information rather than pay the costs of seeking out information on their own (see, e.g., Druckman, Levendusky, & McLain, 2018; Huckfeldt, 2001). Further, this influence of experts in social networks may have intensified as technological advances allow people to spread their thoughts to a wider audience, including those attempting to avoid politics (Settle, 2018). In theory, this seems efficient: those who are interested in politics can inform themselves and pass on the acquired information to their social networks, and those who are uninterested in politics can become informed from these (what we call) political experts, managing to become relatively informed without much cost. Further,

---

[5] We focus on extreme political *preferences* here, which *could* be related to extreme political actions, although we do not examine this.

[6] Although see Carlson (2021), who argues that secondhand exposure to political information through peers often encourages misperceptions.

if it is the case that this setup elevates the electorate's capacity to make sound political decisions, then it is not only efficient but also beneficial to society – improving outcomes for the entire electorate.

However, in practice, this role delegation may instead be harmful to society – leading individuals to make biased decisions and then ultimately to normatively troubling outcomes. Specifically, when experts' preferences diverge from the interests of the broader electorate (Putnam, 2000; 340–342), their power could shift public opinion toward experts' interests at the expense of others. Indeed, experts are not only a leading source of political information, but also a leading source of bias and *mis*information, often communicating inaccurate information and promoting their own interests at their compatriots' expense (Ahn et al., 2014). Even more troubling is the finding that experts are the most common proponents of conspiracy theories (Miller, Saunders, & Farhart, 2016). This evidence suggests that experts, who are often ideologically extreme (Kinder & Kalmoe, 2017) and thus motivated to collect and relay biased information, could lead society to make harmful political decisions – something made possible because of their power in guiding others' political choices.[7]

In this section, we will first discuss the difficulty in studying what we aim to understand – expanding upon this discussion from Sections 1 and 2 but in more detail for our particular research question. Next, we will dive into the theory underlying our research question, which demands the type of design that we use (i.e., randomly assigning motivations). After that, we will present our hypotheses, design, and findings. Last, we will briefly discuss the implications of our findings.

Empirical Quagmire. We aim to understand what occurs when political experts – who have the power to influence others – are extremists who have the motivation to acquire and provide information that could potentially be biased. Phrased another way, we want to know what occurs when extremists have the motivation to acquire political information (i.e., when extremists tend to be experts), as well as when extremists have the motivation to provide political information (i.e., when extremists tend to have low communication costs).[8]

---

[7] Recent research finds that these misperceptions are propagated more by passive – rather than active – information consumption (see Carlson, 2021).

[8] In this Element, we discuss communication costs that include distaste for learning about politics, anxiety about sharing one's political beliefs, and concern over one's reputation (all of which are, on average, lower for the politically interested), although other costs may influence one's likelihood of communicating politically. Nonetheless, communication costs (broadly) are represented in our design and could represent any costs to communication – this is another benefit of our design.

Evaluating this is difficult, however, because the political experts we talk about (i.e., ordinary citizens who are unusually informed about and interested in politics) are self-appointed. Thus, political experts are not only different because they are more ideologically extreme (Kinder & Kalmoe, 2017) but also because they *chose* to be experts, reflecting their asymmetric interest in – and enjoyment of – politics (Hersh, 2020), creating a scenario in which expertise, ideological extremity, and interest go hand in hand in hand (Krupnikov & Ryan, 2022). Consequently, it could be the case that experts' providing of misinformation to the public (for example) is driven by the fact that experts (who are often ideologically extreme and inordinately interested in politics) do not simply synthesize political information in an unbiased manner to their social networks; they seek to *persuade* others rather than *inform* them (see also Ahn et al., 2014).

Thus, our theoretical question is reflected in an empirical quagmire. We want to know if the social capital that political experts hold is beneficial or harmful for society, and we expect that, because experts are often more ideologically extreme and politically interested (i.e., have the motivation to acquire and provide potentially biased information or even misinformation), their power to guide the public leads society to diminished civic capacity. Yet without randomly varying our variables of interest (i.e., these motivations), it is quite possible that correlational findings are driven by self-selection.

To gain traction on this question, we seek to break the self-selection problem through theoretical development and an experiment that focuses on two gaps between extremists and moderates. The first gap, what we call the **expertise gap**, is that between those with more extreme political views (extremists) and those with more moderate views (moderates), where the former (extremists) have more motivation than the latter (moderates) to acquire information. In other words, since experts tend to be extremists, extremists benefit from an expertise gap over moderates because they tend to be more informed than moderates.

The second gap, what we call the **communication gap**, is that between those with the motivation to provide information (i.e., those with low communication costs – the politically interested) and those with*out* the motivation to provide information (i.e., those with high communication costs – the politically *un*interested). In other words, extremists also benefit from a communication gap because their political interest motivates them to provide information more than moderates (who have higher communication costs because they are less interested in politics). After developing a theory explaining how each gap could contribute to individual and collective decision-making and thus societal wellness, we examine the potential effects of each in an incentivized experiment – randomly assigning expertise and communication costs to be uniformly distributed or correlated with extremity. By exogenously assigning these gaps we also exogenously assign motivations, allowing us to examine the extent to which each motivation – that to acquire and provide information – contributes to the quality of individual decisions and collective outcomes.

3.2 Theory

The idea that the social capital of political experts can hurt the electorate in certain contexts is built on three main assumptions. First, people listen to experts – that is, they have the power to influence others. Second, experts are often extremists. And third, extremists often have lower communication costs than does the general public. Before introducing our experimental design, we will demonstrate how the extant literature supports these assumptions and suggests that the proposed problem will continue to get worse with time.[9]

People Listen to Political Experts. Political experts (i.e., ordinary people who are more informed about and interested in politics) hold large amounts of social capital in politics because most people know little about politics (Converse, 1964; Delli Carpini & Keeter, 1996), and therefore often rely on others for political information (Druckman et al., 2018). And perhaps because people overvalue expertise in discussion partners as well as the information needed to make good political decisions (Ahn & Ryan, 2015), the others they typically rely on are their more expert counterparts (Huckfeldt, 2001). Note, however, that while some have argued that political discussions with experts can help those less informed make sound political decisions (Downs, 1957) – as discussed in Section 1 – more recent research finds that this is not necessarily a rational strategy (Lupia & McCubbins, 1998). As noted in previous sections, interpersonal communication with those more politically informed can lead people astray if the informants' preferences are incompatible with the recipients' (Ryan, 2011b). Thus, even though it is not always rational, those with little knowledge often rely on those more expert to guide them in politics (Huckfeldt, 2001).

Political Experts Can Be Extremists. The relationship between expertise and ideological extremity (Kinder & Kalmoe, 2017) is not new – in fact, Zaller (1992) noted that political sophistication helps extremists resist information that counters their predispositions and maintain their political biases. Further,

---

[9] Even if the assumptions do not all *currently* hold, one of the advantages of this type of experiment is the ability to explore what will happen if they hold at some other point in time.

knowledgeable individuals seek out confirmatory information, making doubt, ambivalence, and moderation less likely (Taber & Lodge, 2006).

In the context of interpersonal communication, the fact that experts are often extremists means that those who dominate political discussions are often those who are motivated to send biased information, decreasing the quality of information communicated in these discussions (Ryan, 2011b) – even when voters are motivated to "get it right" (Pietryka, 2016). Indeed, much political discussion is driven not by open-minded listeners seeking information, but by speakers – often ideologically extreme speakers (Huckfeldt & Mendez, 2008) – seeking to persuade or at least express their views (Conover et al., 2002).

In a series of experiments that we also reference in previous sections, for example, Carlson (2018, 2019) demonstrates that information from the media passed on via political discussion is distorted, often containing less information than the original news story. Further, individuals only receive similar information as they would from the news if the information is from someone with similar preferences, but, even in that case, the subjective evaluation of what the information means differs based on whether the information came from another person or from the media (Carlson, 2019). These results make sense when we recall that the goal of many opinion leaders is less to inform others and more to see their views multiplied through their associates – and that the incentive to persuade rather than inform increases with opinion leaders' extremity of views (Ahn et al., 2014).

Extremists Have Relatively Low Communication Costs. While many extremists are politically involved (Krupnikov & Ryan, 2022), interjecting politics into otherwise apolitical discussions, others in the general public either avoid political discussion entirely or participate only enough to gather a sufficient amount of information for the decisions they must make before moving on to more enjoyable topics (Gerber et al., 2012; Huckfeldt & Mendez, 2008; Settle & Carlson, 2019). This is likely because not only are extremists typically more interested in politics than the general public but they also should be more comfortable guiding political discussions because they often have more information than others do (Ahn et al., 2014). In other words, the costs of political communication vary among the public – while most people have high communication costs because discussing politics is burdensome, extremists have low communication costs because they often actually enjoy discussing politics.

This enjoyment of politics has two effects. First, many of these individuals prefer to engage in public opinion leadership via social media, discussion, community organizing, and protest (Hersh, 2020). Second, interest in politics predicts perceived expertise in politics better than actual knowledge (Ryan,

2011a). Hence, individuals who enjoy politics will be motivated to send out political messages and, as noted previously, others will be more willing to accept them.

The Problem Could Get Worse. In advocating for reform to promote social capital, Putnam (2000; 340–342) emphasized that social capital has a dark side: it may produce negative externalities, particularly when that social capital rests primarily in the hands of extremists. Since the time of his writing, several trends have made this scenario more likely.

First, the information age has granted the politically involved more access to political information than ever before. At the same time, it has increased the opportunity costs of obtaining political information due to the greater availability of nonpolitical programming. People with little interest in politics can tune out, avoiding political media to a degree that was difficult when network news dominated primetime (Prior, 2005). Perhaps as a result, expertise is increasingly concentrated among political extremists (Kinder & Kalmoe, 2017) – again, what we refer to as expertise gaps. Obviously, plenty of experts are not extreme and many extremists are not expert. However, whenever expertise gaps exist, they should channel the flow of social capital through to extremists because people seek experts for political information, even when their preferences diverge (Ahn et al., 2014; Huckfeldt, 2001).

Second, the reputational costs of being seen as a political junkie seem to only be increasing over time. Many people are simply uncomfortable discussing politics (Carlson & Settle, 2016; Settle & Carlson, 2019) or dislike others who discuss politics (Druckman et al., 2021; Klar et al., 2018). For these people, political discussion is more costly and hence they are less likely to persuade others and less able to rely on discussion as a shortcut. Like expertise, these communication costs may be correlated with extremity. In fact, Klar and Krupnikov (2016) argue that, as media coverage of partisan politics has become increasingly negative in recent years, the costs of interpersonal communication have increased – except for the most extreme individuals. Again, we refer to this concentration of communication costs among more moderate citizens (and thus low communication costs among the more extreme) as communication gaps. These gaps also give extremists greater social capital because the lower communication costs allow them to play more central roles in discussion networks.

Finally, if individuals produce and maintain social capital through repeated interactions in social networks (Lake & Huckfeldt, 1998), then social media increases experts' ability to gain social capital. Social media allows experts to constantly send out political signals into "news feeds" that are primarily nonpolitical (Settle, 2018). Indeed, one could imagine – and has probably witnessed – individuals building bonding capital with old pictures of holiday parties and support for the local sports teams and then using that capital in an attempt to sway public opinion in one's network. In fact, Krupnikov and Ryan (2022) find that people who believe politics should take a central place in one's life not only post about politics more on social media, they post about *all* topics more frequently.

3.3 Hypotheses

Our core expectation is that both expertise and communication gaps elevate extremists' role in political communication at the expense of moderates and society at large. This expectation leads to various hypotheses, the first set of which predict that extremists will send more information – and moderates will send less information – under expertise or communication gaps. Thus,

Moderate communication hypothesis: Moderates will tend to send *less* information under expertise or communication gaps than in the absence of these gaps.

Extremist communication hypothesis: Extremists will tend to send *more* information under expertise or communication gaps than in the absence of these gaps.

This asymmetric distribution of social capital should shape private returns as well as the externalities. In terms of private returns, both gaps should harm the quality of moderates' decisions. Lacking the human capital that expertise provides, expertise gaps should make moderates more reliant on extremists for information. Yet experts are unlikely to share objective portraits of reality with their more moderate associates. Again, experts are often motivated to send biased messages, choosing to promote their own interests at the expense of their associates (Ahn et al., 2014). And even when they *intend* to provide honest information, they may not be able to separate their factual knowledge from misinformation – experts' higher levels of political interest often motivate them to gather more information, but also more misinformation (Miller et al., 2016). Thus,

Moderate preference hypothesis: Moderates should tend to make lower-quality decisions under expertise or communication gaps than in the absence of these gaps.

These two gaps may help or harm extremists' decisions. Expertise gaps offer extremists greater human capital (in the form of expertise), which should help them adjudicate between competing alternatives and thus make more rational political decisions. Communication gaps, on the other hand, may be *less* beneficial for extremists because people are often too reliant on socially supplied information, even when their personally acquired information is more diagnostic (Ahn & Ryan, 2015). Thus, by playing a more central role in the communication network, extremists may expose themselves to more misinformation.

In terms of externalities, expertise and communication gaps may produce several outcomes as these individual behaviors aggregate into electoral outcomes. On one hand, these gaps may produce offsetting effects, with extremists gaining at the expense of moderates. On the other hand, these gaps may harm *everyone* if social information tends to reduce the quality of extremists' decisions.

Public bad hypothesis: The average quality of collective decisions will be lower under expertise or communication gaps than when expertise and communication costs are randomly distributed.

3.4 Experimental Design

This section's experiment follows our experimental framework outlined in Sections 1 and 2. As we noted previously, the added benefit of this framework for our research question in this section in particular is that we can incorporate uncertainty in politics and varying levels of political expertise. This feature provides an unambiguous means to control the correlation between ideological extremity and expertise within participants' communication networks. Without it, we would not be able to accurately test how extremists' motivation to acquire (and then share) political information influences outcomes.

Thus, here we adopt the basic experimental framework to understand how the distribution of extremism, expertise, and communication costs interacts to influence learning, participation rates, and vote choices. The basic structure of this experiment – building on the basic experimental outline in Section 1's Figure 1 – is summarized in Figure 2. In these elections, groups of twenty-five participate in a maximum of twenty elections over the course of a one-hour session.

3.4.1 Candidates

As in previous experiments, the subjects choose between two candidates who are represented as positions on a scale from one to eleven. The candidate positions are reset after each round, but Candidate A's position is drawn from a uniform distribution between one and seven inclusive, while Candidate B's

GENERAL DESCRIPTION	SECTION 3 EXPERIMENT
Stage 1. The election begins	
Experimental factors assigned	Assigned to groups:
	Control: No expected correlation between extremity and expertise or extremity and communication costs
	Expertise Gap: Positive correlation between extremity and expertise
	Communication Gap: Negative correlation between extremity and communication costs
	Expertise and Communication Gaps: [Positive correlation between extremity and expertise] and [negative correlation between extremity and communication costs]
Candidates' positions assigned	Candidate A: 1–7 Candidate B: 5–11
Participants' positions assigned	One participant at positions 1 and 11 Two at positions 2, 3, 9, and 10 Three at positions 4–8
Stage 2. Private information and first judgment	
Participants view private information Each signal drawn randomly from uniform distribution centered on candidate's true position ± 3	Participants receive 0–2 pieces of private information
After viewing information, participants enter estimates of each candidate's position	
Stage 3. Social information and second judgment	
Participants choose with whom to communicate	Participants choose with whom to send or receive information, or choose not to communicate
	Social information costs assigned at random each election: Some pay five cents to communicate, some pay nothing, some gain five cents
Participants send information	
Participants enter updated estimates of the candidates' positions	
Stage 4. Vote	
Participants vote	Participants must vote for Candidate A, vote for Candidate B, or abstain
Stage 5. Outcome	
Participants learn winner of election and the rewards they received	Participants paid one dollar if they share the position of the winning candidate
The winner of the election determined by majority rule	Pay decreases by ten cents with each unit of distance between positions of participant and the winning candidate
A new election begins at Stage 1	

Figure 2 The stages in an election

position is drawn from a uniform distribution between five and eleven inclusive. The exact positions of the candidates are not known to the voters, creating an incentive to obtain information.

3.4.2 Voters

The subjects (voters) are assigned positions on the same scale such that there is one subject at positions 1 and 11; two at positions 2, 3, 9, and 10; and three at positions 4–8. With these distributions of candidate and voter positions, subjects face a similar challenge as real-world US citizens: relatively moderate citizens must choose between more extreme candidates (Bafumi & Herron, 2010).

The goal of the experimental subjects is to elect the candidate whose position is closest to their own. Each subject's pay decreases by ten cents with each additional unit of distance between their position and the winning candidate's position. If a subject has the same position as the winning candidate, the subject receives one dollar. If the subject is at the opposite end of the scale as the winning candidate, the subject receives nothing.

As noted previously, the information subjects can use to determine the candidates' positions comes in three different forms: publicly available information that is free but of low quality; privately communicated information of higher quality that is randomly assigned to subjects in differing quantities; and socially communicated information taken from other subjects, with the costs of acquiring such information varying between subjects. The public information is the simple ex ante distribution of possible candidate positions. The private and social information require further explanation.

3.4.3 Private Information

At the beginning of each round of voting, subjects receive zero, one, or two pieces of private information. Each piece of private information is a signal about the position of both candidates. These signals are unbiased but noisy – each candidate's signal is a draw from a uniform distribution centered on the candidate's true position and extending three units on either side. Again, we experimentally manipulate the amount of private information each subject receives, as we discuss in detail next.

3.4.4 Social Information

After receiving private information, subjects are given the opportunity to select one fellow subject with whom to communicate. They then choose whether to send information to or request information from this subject. Subjects may also choose not to send or request information.

Subjects then provide social information to anyone they decided to send information to, as well as to anyone requesting information from them. Afterward, subjects receive messages from anyone they requested information from and anyone who elected to send them information. Like private information, these social messages consist of an integer signal about the position of each candidate. Importantly, subjects are *not* required to send signals that conform to the private information they received. Hence, the social information may be *both* biased and noisy.

As explained previously, in the world outside the laboratory some people enjoy political discussion, pursuing it at every chance they get, while others go to great lengths to avoid it and still others generally avoid politics, but use discussion as a shortcut to voting (Gerber et al., 2012; Huckfeldt & Mendez, 2008). Hence the motivation to discuss politics is variable – we account for this tendency by varying the costs of communication among our subjects. Subjects are randomly assigned to pay nothing, pay five cents, or receive five cents to communicate, *regardless* of whether they elect to send or request information.

Subjects vote in fifteen to twenty elections. After each election, the subjects' and candidates' positions are reset and subjects proceed to a new election. After the last election, subjects answer survey questions capturing their various traits.[10] We use this framework to add two election-level treatments, which alter the distributions of expertise and communication costs.

3.4.5 The Treatments

The key motivations we examine in this design are to seek and provide information. Each election, the costs of communication vary between subjects within experimental sessions: to communicate, some will pay a small amount (five cents), others will pay nothing, and the remainder will receive a small payment (five cents). We explore how these costs influence subjects' decisions to send information to and seek information from others, as well as subjects' ability to become informed and vote in their own interests. We expect subjects with lower communication costs (i.e., greater motivation to provide information) to dominate the discussion. In addition to this subject-election-level factor, we also randomly assign two factors at the group level, described next.

Group-Level Factor 1: Expertise Gaps. To examine the consequences of **expertise gaps** – or the elevated motivation of extremists to acquire information – we randomly assign each group of subjects to one of two information treatments that represent stylized versions of the changes in communication costs. Recall that subjects receive zero, one, or two pieces of information and that these information levels are randomly assigned. In the control group for this factor, all subjects have equal probability of having any information level and all information levels are equally likely. Hence, in the control groups, there is no correlation between expertise and extremity in expectation. In the expertise gap treatment, the more ideologically extreme have a greater probability of having more information. The overall distribution of information is the same – one-third with zero pieces of information, one-third with one piece of information, and one-third with two pieces of information – but the expected correlation between ideological extremity and information level is $r = .25$.[11]

---

[10] We gather data on gender, race/ethnicity, and partisan identity because behavior in similar experiments often varies with one's background (see, e.g., Krupnikov et al., 2020). Though we lack the power to estimate heterogeneous treatment effects, our results are unchanged when we condition on these variables in the models.

[11] The exact probabilities are as follows. Ideals 1 & 11: 18.83% 0 pieces; 33.33% 1 piece; 47.84% 2 pieces. Ideals 2 & 10: 25.21% 0 pieces; 33.33% 1 piece; 41.46% 2 pieces. Ideals 3 & 9:

This treatment allows us to compare subjects' ability to learn as the correlation between expertise and ideological extremity increases. If people with little private information in the control are significantly better able to become informed than similar subjects under expertise gaps, it will suggest that the correlation between expertise and ideological extremity hurts learning – that having extremists as informants is detrimental to democracy. If, on the other hand, people under expertise gaps are significantly better able to become informed than similar subjects in the control, it will suggest that instead this correlation between expertise and ideological extremity actually improves rather than hurts learning – that having extremists as informants is beneficial to democracy.

Group-Level Factor 2: Communication Gaps. To explore the implications of **communication gaps** – or the elevated motivation of extremists to provide information – we vary the distribution of information costs across experimental groups. As with private information levels, in the control, there is no expected correlation between communication costs and ideological extremity while, in the communication gap treatment, there is an expected correlation of .25 between communication costs and ideological extremity.

Both the communication and expertise factors – where lower communication costs and higher levels of information are correlated with ideological extremity – should result in networks where subjects with ideologically extreme views dominate information flow. This allows us to examine the impact of extremists' motivations to acquire and provide political information on all subjects' ability to learn and make sound political choices. Combining these two factors in a two-by-two design allows us to separate the effects of each of these two mechanisms.[12]

3.4.6 Sample

We fielded ten experimental sessions from February to May 2018, recruiting subjects from Florida State University's xs/fs subject pool. The subject pool is diverse in terms of race, ethnicity, and major, though, since it is college students, participants tend to be disproportionately young, female, and Democratic

---

31.59% 0 pieces; 33.33% 1 piece; 35.08% 2 pieces. Ideals 4 & 8: 37.97% 0 pieces; 33.33% 1 piece; 28.7% 2 pieces. Ideals 5 & 7: 44.35% 0 pieces; 33.33% 1 piece; 22.32% 2 pieces. Ideal 6: 50.73% 0 pieces; 33.33% 1 piece; 15.94% 2 pieces.

[12] Since these treatments affect electorate-level distributions of expertise and communication costs, we must assign them at the group-election level rather than at the subject level. As a consequence, we have the statistical power to examine the independent effects of each treatment, but lack the power to estimate their interactive effects since interactions require far more statistical power (see Maxwell, Delaney, & Kelley, 2017; 342).

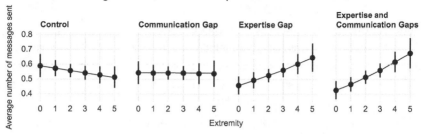

Figure 3 In expertise gap elections, extremists dominate the supply of information.

relative to the population of US adults. For details on sample demographics, see Section A1 of the Supporting Information (SI). In each experimental session, subjects completed as many elections as they could over the course of an hour, up to a maximum of 20 elections. Thus, our sample includes 250 subjects (10 sessions × 25 subjects per session) who completed a combined total of 188 elections, yielding 4,700 observations at the subject-election level (25 subjects/session × 188 elections).

Before the elections began, participants learned the rules and baseline incentives and then completed one training election. After the training election, participants completed a comprehension quiz (for details on the quiz, see SI-A2). They began the elections used for the analysis only after affirming that they understood the correct answers. SI-A3 displays screenshots and the instructions given to all participants.

3.5 Experimental Findings

We begin by examining the effects of the expertise and communications gap treatments on individuals. We first examine how expertise and communication gaps affect the extent to which extremists dominate the supply of information. We then examine how expertise and communication gaps affect the ability of moderates and extremists to support the candidates who best represent their views. Finally, we shift to election-level results to see the aggregated consequences of these two gaps.

Exchanging Information. Again, the subjects were able to provide information in two ways. First, they could choose to send information to another subject. Second, one or more fellow subjects could request information from them. As a result, subjects sent between zero and six messages in an election (mean = 1.5 messages; standard deviation = 0.7). Figure 3 shows the expected number of messages each subject sent in an election as a function of their extremity, which equals their absolute distance from the median voter. In the control elections, moderates sent roughly the same number of messages as extremists. The same was true for the communication gaps elections. In the expertise gaps elections, however, the extremists dominated the conversation. In these elections, the most extreme subjects were expected to send about 0.25 more messages than the most moderate subjects (Figure 4), which reflects about a 40 percent increase.

These results provide partial support for the communication hypotheses. As expected, moderates provided less information in the expertise gap treatment than in the control, while extremists provided more. But the communication gap treatment did not provide a similar effect. What happened? As Figure 5A demonstrates, the communication gap treatment *did* increase extremists' tendency to choose communication over isolation. However, the reduced communication costs under the communication gap treatment caused extremists to *request* more information from others (Figure 5B and 5C).

This is potentially a problem because, in expectation, the social information is biased while the private information is not. If these extremists then rely on their socially acquired information, it will lead to worse decisions.

Decision Quality. After acquiring information, subjects identify which candidate they want to win. We use this information to evaluate the quality of subjects' decisions by differentiating between correct and incorrect preferences. In real-world settings, correct preferences are difficult to determine, but, in our study, they are unambiguously measured as a preference for the candidate closest to the subject because this candidate maximizes the subject's payment.[13] By focusing on preferences rather than vote choice, we are able to include participants who chose to abstain, avoiding one source of posttreatment bias.

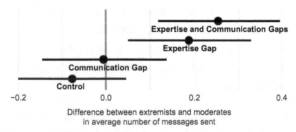

Figure 4 The marginal effect of extremity on communication levels is greatest in elections with the expertise gap treatment.

Note: The plots display mean estimates and 95 percent confidence intervals based on ten thousand posterior simulations from the multilevel negative binomial regression displayed in SI-A3, Table 5, Model 1.

---

[13] Subjects equally close to each candidate are omitted from this analysis.

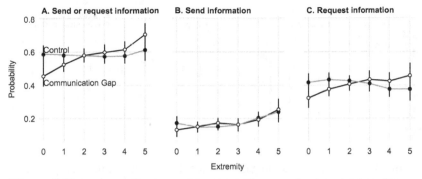

Figure 5 The communication gap treatment increased extremists' tendency to communicate and decreased moderates' tendency to communicate. These patterns were driven primarily by requesting information (Panel C) rather than choosing to send information (Panel B).

Note: In each election, each subject chooses whether they wish to send information, request information, or neither. The plots display the mean behavior of all subjects at each level of extremity under the control condition (light grey) or in the communication gap treatment (dark grey). The vertical lines indicate 95 percent confidence intervals.

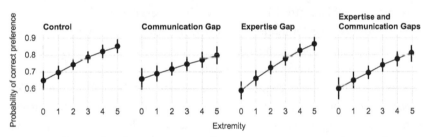

Figure 6 Extremists form correct preferences at greater rates than moderates.

Figure 6 plots the probability that each subject formed a correct preference. In all experimental groups, more extreme subjects are more likely to form a correct preference, but this relationship is particularly strong under expertise gaps and weakest under communication gaps.

Figure 7 plots the treatment effects by subjects' extremity. The Y-axis displays the change in a subject's probability of forming a correct preference, relative to the control.[14] The left panel of the figure demonstrates that more extreme subjects do worse in communication gap elections than in control elections. The opposite pattern emerges in expertise gap elections, where it is moderates who do worse than they do in control elections. These effects do not offset each other in elections with both communication and expertise gaps.

---

[14] Change in probability = p(correct|extremity,treatment) − p(correct|extremity,control).

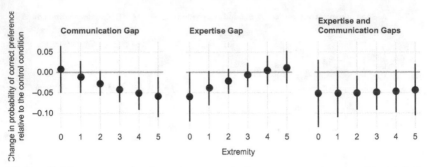

Figure 7 The communication gap treatment hurts more extreme subjects (left panel) while the expertise gap treatment hurts more moderate subjects (middle panel). Everyone tends to be worse off in elections featuring both treatments (right panel).

Note: The plots display mean estimate and 95 percent confidence intervals based on ten thousand posterior simulations from the multilevel logistic regression displayed in SI-A3, Table 5, Model 2.

Instead, *everyone* tends to do worse in these elections relative to control elections, though the effect is not statistically significant for the most moderate or most extreme subjects (for whom we have the fewest observations).

These results reveal a more complicated pattern than our hypotheses predicted. Recall that the *moderate preference hypothesis* predicted that moderates would tend to make lower-quality decisions under expertise and/or communication gaps than in the control. We see support for this expectation under expertise gaps, but we do *not* see support for it under communication gaps. Rather than aiding extremists at the expense of moderates, communication gaps – that is, when extremists are motivated to communicate with other participants – served to harm *extremists* by exposing them to more misinformation. This result provides an early sign that expertise and communication gaps produce externalities. To better examine this possibly, we shift our unit of analysis to the election level.

Election Outcomes. Putnam (2000; 19) emphasized that social capital affects outcomes for both individuals and groups. We have looked at the former – individuals' welfare – and next we look at the latter – the group's welfare. For this outcome, we examine the effects of expertise and communication gaps on the vote share of the candidate that is best for the group as a whole. In the experiment, this candidate is always the one closest to the median voter because it maximizes profit for the group.[15]

Recall that we offered two competing expectations. If expertise and communication gaps help extremists at the expense of moderates, the average quality

---

[15] We exclude from analysis elections in which the candidates are equally close to the median.

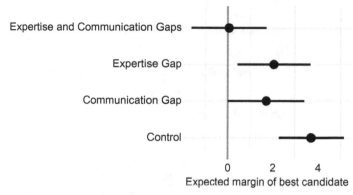

Figure 8 Negative externalities under expertise and communication gaps

of collective decisions should remain similar under expertise or communication gaps compared to the decisions made in the absence of these gaps. Alternatively, concentrating social capital among extremists may harm the community as a whole. And thus the *public bad hypothesis* posits that the average quality of collective decisions will be lower under these gaps than in their absence.

Figure 8 plots the expected vote margin for the best candidate[16] for each of the treatment groups. In control elections, the best candidate tends to win by about a three-vote margin. In elections under expertise gaps *or* communication gaps, this margin shrinks to a single vote. In elections under *both* expertise *and* communication gaps, this margin shrinks to zero. Figure 9 demonstrates that the best candidate's expected margin is significantly lower under the expertise gap and communication gap elections than in the control. The expected margin is even lower in elections with both treatments than in elections with only one treatment.

Thus, our evidence is consistent with the *public bad hypothesis*. We see the welfare of the electorate as a whole diminishes when extremists hold and share the most information. In other words, the social capital they hold produces negative externalities.

3.6 Conclusion

We began this section with the observation that political experts have the ability to influence the general public, but that experts are often biased extremists

---

[16] The expected vote margin is as follows: (number of votes for best candidate) − (number of votes for the other candidate).

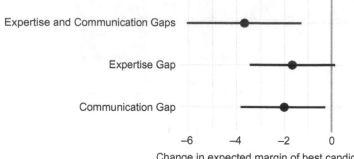

Figure 9 Expertise and communication gaps reduce the expected vote margin for the best candidate.

Note: The plots display mean estimate and 95 percent confidence intervals based on ten thousand posterior simulations from the multilevel linear regression displayed in SI-A3, Table 5, Model 3.

with low communication costs – that is, that they have the motivation to acquire and share biased political information. Our experiment investigates the consequences of this by exogenously manipulating motivations to acquire and share political information – randomly assigning these two motivations to those with extreme or not extreme preferences.

Our findings in this experiment suggest a number of troubling consequences. First, political experts have disproportionate power in a democracy – they are not just one person, one vote because they guide others' political decisions as well as make their own (see also Katz, 1957). Second, low-knowledge individuals are not necessarily able to learn about politics from their better-informed associates, giving less clout to recommendations from Downs (1957) for those less informed to rely on the better informed to make decisions. Third, and last, interpersonal communication – within the context of experts' role as both information providers and extremists with low communication costs – can be detrimental to democratic decisions: worse decisions are made when extremists are the source of information. In particular, we see that when those with more extreme preferences are motivated to acquire and share information, there is more bias in social signals, fewer moderate subjects identifying the candidate that will offer them a larger payoff, and, ultimately, a decreased vote share for the candidate who offers the best overall payoff to the electorate as a whole.

These findings are consistent with previous survey research that suggests that perceived experts dominate discussion (Huckfeldt, 2001), have larger influence on vote choices (Ryan, 2011a), and can spread misinformation (Miller et al., 2016), and thus lead us to question the Downsian (1957) model of trickle-down political information. Given experts' interest in politics and tendency toward extremism and bias, their power to guide others is troubling, as our results demonstrate. A requirement of a properly functioning deliberative democracy is mutual respect – a requirement that is easier met in theory than in practice (Sanders, 1997). The deliberative democracy in our laboratory failed to meet this requirement, as the increased social capital of experts meant they received more respect than others. The willingness of some experts to mislead their fellow participants demonstrates that they showed less respect to those participants.

Our results from this experiment are also timely, as social media has allowed for greater communication between citizens than ever before. That communication has some obvious potential benefits – for example, increased voter turnout (Bond et al., 2012) – but scholars have also noted drawback – for example, increased dislike of outpartisans (Settle, 2018) or increased ideological extremity (Bail et al., 2018). Here, we see negative consequences of increased communication can occur even in the absence of partisanship and ideology. The cause of these negative consequences is the willingness of individuals to trust experts who often have positions at the extremes, even though these experts have incentives to misinform and mislead.

These findings could not have been discovered without an approach that accounts for motivations by exogenously assigning them – our design allowed us to isolate mechanisms that might otherwise remain hopelessly entangled. It allowed us to demonstrate that the efficacy of political communication indeed hinges on participants' motivations. Yet, while the experiment featured in this section demonstrates how particular motivations in interpersonal communication can have deleterious effects on society, the experiment featured in the next section highlights a motivation that can promote more beneficial effects.

4 Motivating Prosociality

The results in the previous section align with the recent experimental research discussed in Section 2 about informal, everyday political discussion. These results cast doubt on interpersonal communication's ability to help participants make better political decisions. Yet the results seem incongruent with theories of deliberative democracy, which argue that an open and honest conversation enables individuals to exchange distinctive insights while expelling their misconceptions (e.g., Esterling, Neblo, & Lazer, 2011; Neblo, 2015).

Thus, at first glance, the literatures on informal discussion and formal deliberation seem to suggest opposite conclusions about the efficacy of interpersonal communication. Yet this apparent contradiction is at least partially illusory, as deliberative theorists do not expect these benefits to accrue in *all* conversations, but rather in specific formal or idealized settings (e.g., Habermas, 1975). But tension remains between these literatures, perhaps partly because people have invested great resources to promote deliberation in real-world settings. Many scholars, foundations, and citizen groups dedicate countless time, money, and energy toward improving communication between citizens. Unless these efforts can create real-world conditions that mimic the idealized settings examined in deliberative research, our findings in Section 3 suggest that these investments may only propagate the interests of experts rather than the broader community.

One means to address this challenge is to identify the mechanisms that make interpersonal communication more or less deliberative. In other words, it is possible that much of the apparent conflict between these literatures arises because they focus on different contexts that impose different sets of motivations – again, examining which motivations lead to which outcomes in interpersonal communication is one of the aims of this Element. In the previous section, we focused on motivations to send and receive information and discovered that these motivations – when held by extremists – lead to deleterious consequences for individuals and the broader group. In this section, we turn to three other motivations, all drawn from the psychological theories of motivated reasoning: partisan, accuracy, and prosocial motivations.

While political scientists have long paid attention to partisan motivations, and recently have paid attention to accuracy motivations, little work has examined prosocial motivations. We believe that these prosocial motivations – which reflect desires to help others in addition to oneself – are an essential element of formal deliberation, but are also common during informal political discussion, which typically occurs among friends and family (Klofstad et al., 2009; Mutz, 2006). Further, we believe that these motivations could significantly improve the efficacy of discussion by helping both senders and receivers make better choices. By paying insufficient attention to these motivations, then, previous work has overlooked a key mechanism that may make informal communication more effective and increase collective civic capacity.

4.1 Background

Informal political discussion most frequently arises as a byproduct of everyday interaction (Carlson & Settle, 2022). Rather than a purposive search for political information, conversations about seemingly apolitical topics occasionally drift to political matters, if only for a moment. When asked, people often state that they talk about politics to pass time, rather than as a conscious attempt to gain information or persuade others (Eveland et al., 2011; 1091). As a result, political discussion typically occurs among friends, family, coworkers, or other groups who frequently interact with one another (Huckfeldt, Johnson, & Sprague, 2004; Klofstad et al., 2009; Mutz, 2006).

When political discussion occurs as an inadvertent consequence of interaction with friends and family, the strategic goals that previous research has focused on may be absent. In these situations, people should be more likely to communicate with empathy for their discussion partners. Indeed, ethnographic research on informal discussion emphasizes empathy. Walsh (2004), for example, met with several groups who gather informally to talk about life, the weather, and occasionally politics. Her careful observations and interviews suggest that political discussion often arises as a byproduct of conversation about seemingly apolitical topics. These conversations occur only because participants feel a sense of shared interests with each other, and these shared interests foster a sense of responsibility to fellow group members (Walsh, 2004; 183). Thus, even when disagreement arises, this responsibility should help people set their predispositions aside, allowing them to hear alternative perspectives with more clarity and offer advice with less bias.

Though shared interests may discourage biased communication, people do not always communicate with complete honesty. People regularly mislead each other in conversations, most frequently with casual acquaintances rather than close friends and family (DePaulo & Kashy, 1998). Yet they are also less likely to pretend to agree with casual acquaintances than friends and family (DePaulo & Kashy, 1998). Perhaps for this reason, political discussion with casual acquaintances such as coworkers often leads to disagreement (Mutz & Mondak, 2006). Such conversations may best reflect the strategic, persuasive environments highlighted in past experimental research. In these scenarios – with casual acquaintances where there are fewer prosocial motivations – people might be more willing to hide relevant information in order to persuade others or win an argument.

Though disagreement may be most common among casual acquaintances, it still arises among more intimate associates. Since people *discuss* politics most frequently with friends and family, they also routinely *disagree* about politics with friends and family (Eveland, Appiah, & Beck, 2017). Nonetheless, the *reasons* the disagreement arises in such conversations may differ and therefore the *effects* of such disagreement may differ as well. With stronger feelings of mutual responsibility, people may be less compelled to win the argument. Still, though, disagreement can cause people to dig in their heels – and, when they do, they may become more critical of evidence that runs against their predispositions and therefore less likely to learn from the encounter (Kunda, 1990). Work on motivated reasoning suggests that people often reinterpret the information they receive to conform to their prior beliefs (Lodge & Taber, 2013). Feelings of mutual responsibility may not be sufficient to overcome these biases. Therefore, understanding when informal discussion will be most beneficial requires a theory explaining how individual motivations – such as partisan, accuracy, and prosocial motivations – influence interpersonal communication.

4.2 Theory

Motivations are the goals one hopes to satisfy when forming an evaluation or reaching a decision. They determine whether and how one searches for information, whether one notices peripheral information, how one evaluates information, and whether perceived information influences judgments or behaviors. Among the many goals someone may hold, the most commonly studied in politics are partisan motivations, also known as directional or defense motivations. Partisan motivations encourage cursory, biased information searches and reliance on mental shortcuts to process information (Kunda, 1990). In comparison, accuracy motivations activate more effortful processing, encouraging people to seek more information and employ more complex reasoning strategies (e.g., Baumeister & Newman, 1994; Tetlock, 1985). Real-world political discussions in particular feature a mix of motivations, which vary in intensity. Although previous research has not thoroughly examined the psychological mechanisms driving the efficacy of discussion, participants in prior experiments behave much like they would with partisan motivations (Huckfeldt, Pietryka, & Reilly, 2014; 121).

However, other motivations are likely present in discussions. In particular, though absent in previous laboratory experiments, *prosocial* motivations may be prominent in real-world discussions. Prosocial motivations reflect one's desire to help others. This desire arises when people empathize with one another (Batson, 2016; Batson et al., 2008), often because they are socially close and share positive experiences (Preston & Waal, 2002). Thus, such feelings should arise most often in political discussions among close friends and family rather than conversations with neighbors, coworkers, or other casual acquaintances. Yet experimental participants do not know the identities of their discussants, and therefore many of the constraints imposed by close, personal relationships are absent in experimental settings. Without the feelings of empathy, affection, and trust common among intimate associates, previous experiments often best approximate conversations between neighbors, coworkers, or other casual acquaintances.[17]

How might the experimental results change if participants hold stronger prosocial motivations akin to those held between intimate associates? If motivations determine how people seek and process information, the nature of political discussion should differ when discussants' motivations diverge from those elicited in previous studies. As we have noted, motivations should govern each outcome that discussion research typically examines – this includes who people seek as informants, the magnitude of bias in the messages that informants provide, and ultimately whether communication promotes more accurate judgments and better decisions.

4.3 Hypotheses

Motivations Govern Information Seeking. As noted previously, when studying who people communicate with, informal discussion scholars often draw from Downs (1957): they assess the informants' expertise and preferences. Though individuals would prefer informants with high levels of expertise and shared preferences, such informants are rare. When forced to choose between expertise and shared preferences, both observational (Huckfeldt, 2001) and experimental work (Ahn et al., 2013; Ahn & Ryan, 2015) suggest citizens prioritize expertise. Yet it is likely that in real-world discussion, the informant qualities individuals care about depends on the individuals' motivations. Indeed, when people care about others' well-being (De Dreu, Weingart, & Kwon, 2000; Grant & Berry, 2011), or offer advice to those they care about (Jonas & Frey, 2003), they search for information from a more diverse set of perspectives than they would if purely self-interested. Thus,

Diverse information hypothesis: People with stronger prosocial motivations will seek informants whose preferences tend to be *less* similar to their own.

---

[17] Though most common in close relationships, prosocial motivations can also reflect the desire to help unknown others. Dalton (2008) argues that feelings of obligation toward others provide an important source of civic duty (see also Mullinix, 2018). Thus, work on civic duty can help us understand how prosocial motivations might affect information processing outside of laboratory settings. Kam (2007) argues that civic duty encourages people to think harder about political candidates, seek information in a more evenhanded manner, and think more carefully about the information they receive. Mullinix (2018) shows that encouraging civic duty tends to increase partisans' self-reported willingness to discuss politics with members of the opposing political party. These effects align nicely with psychology research on prosocial motivations as well as suggest that prosocial motivations could influence interpersonal communication, but this work has yet to disentangle the consequences of prosocial motivations from other components of civic duty, which include feelings of autonomy and commitment to social order (Dalton, 2008).

Motivations Govern Message Bias. After exploring information seeking, experimental research often examines the messages informants provide. Much as Downs expects, this work shows that informants send increasingly biased messages as their preferences diverge from their discussant (Ahn et al., 2013; Huckfeldt et al., 2014). But informants motivated to help their discussants should be better able to put their own interests aside, encouraging them to send less biased messages. Therefore,

Bias hypothesis: People with stronger prosocial motivations will tend to be *less* biased in their communications.

Motivations Govern the Efficacy of Communication. To evaluate the usefulness of communication, past work has typically focused on whether communication helps people form more accurate judgments and vote correctly. As explained previously, this work defines a correct vote as one where an individual selects the candidate who best matches their preferences or interests (e.g., Ryan, 2011b; Sokhey & McClurg, 2012). Under these criteria, people often fail to benefit from communication. By overvaluing expertise, they receive biased information, but rely on it nonetheless. This biased information clouds their candidate evaluations and often leads them to support candidates whose positions are in opposition to their own (Ahn & Ryan, 2015).

Prosocial motivations should encourage people to help others, but may also allow them to better help themselves. Indeed, the deliberative democracy literature posits that deliberation should help participants clarify their own needs, improving their ability to advance their interests (Mendelberg, 2002; 173). As Warren (1992; 12) argues, "By raising one's wants, needs, and desires to the level of consciousness and by formulating them in speech, one increases one's sense of identity and autonomy – aside from any advantages that might accrue from the substantive outcomes of collective decisions."

A large body of social psychological experiments supports this notion. People consider information more carefully when others depend on their advice (Jonas, Schulz-Hardt, & Frey, 2005) or when they expect to justify their decisions to others (Tetlock, 1985). This effortful, objective processing allows people to make better predictions and better assess their own uncertainty (Tetlock & Kim, 1987). But these benefits are unlikely to arise when individuals are unconcerned about the opinion or well-being of their discussants because they lack sufficient incentive for self-reflection. In contrast, those with prosocial motivations should benefit in their own decisions from this careful, objective processing. Thus,

Correct voting hypothesis 1: People with stronger prosocial motivations will be *more* likely to vote for the candidate that best represents their views.

The informal discussion literature has typically defined correct voting in terms of individuals' own interests, but deliberative theorists may expect discussion to promote a more collectivistic voting pattern. Many deliberation scholars assert that deliberation broadens individual interests to include the public good. Mendelberg (2002; 156) summarizes this view. "Talk can create a norm of group-interest in which individuals come to see their own self-interest as consonant with the self-interest of every other member of the group. This norm in turn causes individuals to act with the goal of maximizing the group's interest." Indeed, when individuals perceive their well-being to depend on the well-being of others, they are more likely to work toward the group's interests (Batson & Shaw, 1991; De Dreu & Boles, 1998; Grant, 2007). Hence,

Correct voting hypothesis 2: People with stronger prosocial motivations will be *more* likely to vote for the candidate who best represents the group.

If these motivations influence individuals' own judgments and the bias in the messages they send, they should also influence the extent to which their communications are helpful to others. Thus, if prosocial motivations improve judgments and reduce message bias, then,

Prosocial informant hypothesis: People whose *informants* hold stronger prosocial motivations will be *more* likely to vote correctly.

4.4 Experimental Design

To examine our expectations, we seek to make only subtle changes to the experimental framework that previous informal political communication has relied on – including the experiment we reported in Section 3. Specifically, we add small incentives to encourage different motivations. In this experiment, groups of seven participants play up to fifteen election rounds. Each stage in an election is summarized in Figure 10.

Before describing the rest of the design, we must emphasize that our aim is *not* to test deliberative democratic theory, but rather to examine how individual motivations make communication more or less deliberative. Therefore, we do not directly examine important elements of deliberation such as diversity of viewpoints or equality. Indeed, no research design can evaluate deliberative democracy in its entirety if one adopts a comprehensive view of deliberation. For instance, Neblo (2015) conceives of deliberative democracy as a system that includes facially deliberative practices like formal deliberative forums, but also encompasses a broad set of outcomes including personal cognition and interpersonal discussion. He advocates for more research examining how

GENERAL DESCRIPTION	SECTION 4 EXPERIMENT
Stage 1. The election begins	
Experimental factors assigned	Assigned to individuals:
	Control condition: receive only the baseline incentives
	Prosocial motivations: baseline incentives + paid when fellow participants who request information from them vote correctly
	Partisan motivations: baseline incentives + assigned a candidate (A or B) and paid more if that candidate wins
	Accuracy motivations: baseline incentives + paid for each candidate whose position they can correctly identify at Stage 3
Candidates' positions assigned	Candidate A: 1–6 Candidate B: 2–7
Participants' positions assigned	One participant at each position 1–7
Stage 2. Private information and first judgment	
Participants view private information Each signal drawn randomly from uniform distribution centered on candidate's true position ± 3	Participants receive 0–4 pieces of private information
After viewing information, participants enter estimates of each candidate's position	
Stage 3. Social information and second judgment	
Participants choose whom to communicate with	Participants choose whom to request information from
	Social information is always free
Participants send information	
Participants enter updated estimates of the candidates' positions	
Stage 4. Vote	
Participants vote	Participants must vote for Candidate A or Candidate B
Stage 5. Outcome	
Participants learn winner of election and the rewards they received The winner of the election determined by majority rule	Participants gain fifty cents when the candidate closest to their own position wins, lose fifty cents when this candidate loses, and neither gain nor lose when equally close to each candidate
A new election begins at Stage 1	

Figure 10 The stages in an election

these broader, more indirect aspects of the deliberative system can perform deliberative functions (Neblo, 2015; 29). Focusing only on facially deliberative practices, he argues, can obscure the role that indirectly deliberative practices play in achieving deliberative ends (Neblo, 2015; 47–48).

4.4.1 Candidates

As usual, each election was a competition between two computer-generated candidates. In this experiment, the candidates' positions were integers drawn at random from uniform distributions. Candidate A's distribution ranged from one to six and B's from two to seven. Candidate A's expected position under this distribution was 3.5 and B's was 4.5.

4.4.2 Voters

Before each election, participants were likewise assigned a position on the same scale. Each of the seven participants in a group received a unique integer position ranging from one to seven. Participants gained fifty cents when the candidate closest to their own position won, lost fifty cents when this candidate lost, and neither gained nor lost when they were equally close to each candidate. And, again, participants knew with certainty their own positions, but had to learn about the *candidates'* positions through private and social information.

4.4.3 Private Information

Much like real-world citizens and the participants highlighted in Section 3, participants in this experiment varied in their levels of expertise. At the start of each election, each participant received between zero and four pieces of private information.[18] Each piece of private information provided an integer signal about each candidate's position. Each signal was drawn randomly from a uniform distribution ranging from three units in either direction from the candidate's true position. Just like the signals discussed in Section 3, these signals were thus unbiased, but noisy: the expected signal reflected a candidate's true position, but many signals differed from this quantity. After receiving private information, participants entered an estimate of each candidate's position.

4.4.4 Social Information

Similar to the participants featured in Section 3, participants could then request information from one of the other six participants in their group or they could instead choose not to seek social information. When requesting social information, participants were shown their potential informants' positions and levels of expertise. If a fellow participant requested social information, the sender was shown the requester's position and levels of expertise. In this case, the sender must then send a message to the requester about the position of each candidate in the form of an integer signal about the position of each candidate. Again, though, these signals were not required to reflect their true beliefs. Nor were participants required to provide the same signals to all participants

---

[18] Expertise levels varied randomly within groups and elections (as compared to the experiments examined in Section 3, where expertise levels were correlated with extremism in the treatment group). In each election, one participant in each group received four pieces of private information, two participants received three, one participant received two, two participants received one, and one participant received zero.

who requested information from them.[19] After participants exchanged social information, they entered (potentially) updated estimates of the candidates' positions and then cast their votes. Since our interest for this study focuses most directly on the choices participants make rather than the composition of the electorate, we ensure all participants cast votes by eliminating the choice to abstain.

4.4.5 Treatments

Some participants, henceforth the **control condition**, received only the incentives just explained. To see how elevated prosocial motivations change behavior, however, the experiment also randomly assigned additional incentives. To encourage **prosocial motivations**, some participants were paid when fellow participants who requested information from them voted correctly. These participants gained twenty-five cents for each requester who subsequently voted for the correct candidate (i.e., the candidate whose position was closest to the requester's position), but lost twenty-five cents for each requester who voted incorrectly. When the candidates were equally proximate to the requester, the participant neither gained nor lost money as a result of the requester's vote. Participants were never aware of fellow participants' incentives, aside from the common goal of electing the closest candidate.

The control condition was not motivation free, but rather provided the same incentives used in previous research (see, e.g., Ahn et al., 2013, 2010; Huckfeldt et al., 2014; Pietryka, 2016) and therefore encouraged the same partisan and accuracy motivations. To clarify the meaning of these motivations, the experiment also randomly assigned additional incentives to some participants to elevate these motivations. To encourage **partisan motivations**, some participants received an additional fifty cents if Candidate A won the election and others received this if Candidate B won. To encourage **accuracy motivations**, some participants received twenty-five cents for correctly identifying the position of one candidate and fifty cents for correctly identifying the positions of both candidates in their final judgments.

The motivation treatments were randomly assigned to participants and persisted for five elections, after which new incentives were assigned. All groups participated in five elections in which some of their members received partisan and accuracy incentives, five with partisan and prosocial incentives, and

---

[19] Previous work has allowed participants to deny their fellow participants' information requests. Yet, in these experiments, participants almost always provide information, denying less than 5 percent of requests (Ahn et al., 2013; Huckfeldt et al., 2014; Pietryka, 2016). Thus, providing the opportunity to deny requests provides insufficient variation to be of interest yet adds endogeneity to the design.

five with accuracy and prosocial incentives.[20] The randomization allowed participants to receive multiple motivation treatments at once because real-world motivations are not mutually exclusive. Even the strongest partisans sometimes desire accurate beliefs, casting away their predispositions when lacking sufficient supporting evidence (Kunda, 1990; 483). Similarly, prosocial motivations encourage information seeking, in part, by elevating accuracy goals (Jonas & Frey, 2003).

In all elections, two participants in each group were in the control condition and the remaining five received additional incentives. In elections featuring partisan and accuracy incentives, four participants in each group received partisan incentives, equally divided between Candidate A and Candidate B. One individual from each party and one "nonpartisan" also received accuracy incentives. In elections featuring partisan and prosocial incentives, the same distribution was used with prosocial in place of accuracy incentives. In elections featuring accuracy and prosocial incentives, two participants had prosocial incentives, one had accuracy incentives, and two had both.

4.4.6 Sample

We fielded six sessions of this study in spring 2016 with 126 participants, again recruited from Florida State University's xs/fs subject pool. For details on sample demographics, see the online supporting information, SI-B. At the start of each session, participants were assigned to a seven-person group. Each group completed up to 15 elections during the ninety-minute session, yielding a total of 270 completed elections and 1,890 subject-election-level observations (7 subjects per group × 270 elections).

Like the experiment covered in Section 3, participants voted in one training election prior to beginning the elections used for analysis. After the training election, they completed a comprehension quiz (see SI-B2). SI-B2 displays screenshots from the elections and instructional materials given to all participants.

4.5 Experimental Findings

The analyses follow the order of an election. In Section 3, most treatments were assigned at the group level and thus the analysis focused on group outcomes. In this experiment, however, the treatments were assigned at the individual level and we therefore focus on the behavior of individual participants. We first examine how prosocial motivations affect who participants seek for

---

[20] Each group encountered these three sets of elections in random order.

information and then the messages participants provide. We then examine if prosocial motivations influence whether the communicated messages improve vote decisions.

Information Seeking. Each election, participants chose from whom to seek social information, typically deciding based on their potential informants' expertise and positions. As noted earlier, previous work suggests expertise trumps shared positions as a selection criterion, but motivations may change the relative influence of each. To estimate how participants' motivations condition the effects of these criteria, we next examine the dyadic relationships between participants and each of their six potential informants in an election. Using a conditional logit (Greene, 2012; 766–767), we regress an indicator of whether the participant requested information from the potential informant on this potential informant's (1) absolute ideological distance from the participant's position and (2) expertise level.[21] The model interacts these variables with indicators for the participants' motivations. Figure 11 displays the model estimates.

In Figure 11, the negative coefficient associated with distance shows that participants in the control condition tend to prefer informants with preferences similar to their own – after controlling for potential informants' expertise. The interaction terms associated with distance indicate that this tendency is weaker for participants with prosocial or accuracy motivations than for those

DV = Whether the participant requested information from the potential informant

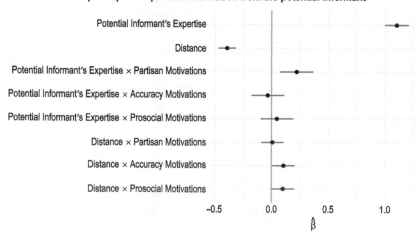

Figure 11 Coefficients from a conditional logistic regression show that participants seek information from less distant, more expert informants.

---

in the control condition. For participants in the control condition, each unit of distance on the seven-point policy space decreases the log odds that the participant requests information from this potential informant by 0.4. For participants with prosocial motivations, however, each additional unit of distance decreases the log odds of a request by only 0.3 (first difference = 0.1, $p = .05$). In other words, participants with elevated prosocial motivations tended to seek more diverse informants – supporting the *diverse information hypothesis*.

The positive coefficient associated with expertise shows that participants prefer more expert informants – after controlling for preference differences. For participants in the control condition, the figure shows that each additional piece of private information a potential informant receives increases the log odds of the participant requesting information from them by 1.1. Participants with prosocial motivations did not differ from those in the control condition in their preference for expertise. Thus, when seeking more diverse views, participants with elevated prosocial motivations did not sacrifice expertise. In contrast, participants with partisan motivations placed a *greater* emphasis on the potential informant's expertise than did those in the control condition.

Taken together, the results in Figure 11 suggest that participants with partisan motivations become more Downsian in their selection of informants than those in the control condition, while participants with accuracy or prosocial motivations become less Downsian. By placing a lower premium on shared preferences, those with accuracy or prosocial motivations encounter more of the cross-cutting communication that deliberative theorists seek.

Message Bias. How did motivations impact the information participants sent? Their incentive to elect the most proximate candidate encouraged them to send biased information. Our design allows us to measure message bias by comparing the absolute difference between the participant's self-reported belief about the candidate's position and the signal the participant sent about the candidate's position. Since each message included a signal about both candidates, we take the average bias of these two signals. The *bias hypothesis* predicts this bias will be weaker for those with prosocial motivations.

To explore these expectations, Figure 12 plots coefficients from a regression where the outcome is the absolute difference between the sender's message and their belief about the position of a candidate. The baseline coefficients show the average message bias for each set of motivations, with the intercept displaying the average in the control condition and each beta coefficient showing the offset for a given set of motivations. As expected, participants tend to send

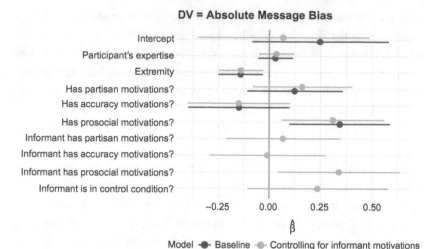

Figure 12 Participants with prosocial motivations send less biased messages than those in the control condition.

biased messages, but participants with prosocial motivations send less biased messages than do those in the control condition.[22]

The coefficients from the model with interactions examine whether motivations attenuate the relationship between ideological distance and message bias. Figure 13 shows the predicted values from this model. Participants send increasingly biased messages as the recipient's position diverges from their own. For participants in the control condition, each additional unit of distance increases message bias by about one-third of a unit on the seven-point scale. This effect is half as strong for participants with prosocial motivations, however.[23] Prosocial motivations do not eliminate message bias, but they do attenuate the effect of distance, indicating that prosocial motivations can improve the quality of cross-cutting discourse by minimizing biased signals. Interestingly, partisan motivations do not *magnify* bias beyond the effects of distance observed in other treatments, suggesting the control condition already incentivized partisan motivated behavior.

Voting. Voting represents the final decision participants make in each election. As previously discussed, informal discussion research often focuses on an individualistic conception of correct voting while the deliberation literature often focuses on a more collectivistic conception. Our design provides an opportunity to explore how motivations affect correct voting under both definitions.

---

[22] Average Bias$_{Prosocial}$ = 1.2; Average Bias$_{Control}$ = 1.5; first difference = -0.3, p < .01.

[23] The slope is significantly weaker for participants with prosocial motivations than for those in the control (first difference = 0.14, p = .02).

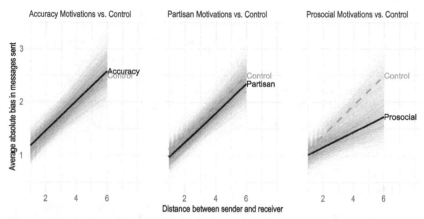

Figure 13 Message bias increases with distance between sender and receiver. This tendency is weaker for participants with elevated prosocial motivations.

Recall that individualistic correct voting occurs when a participant selects the candidate whose position is closest to their own – this candidate always maximizes the participant's profit, regardless of other motivations. Collectivistic correct voting occurs when a participant selects the candidate most proximate to the median voter, because electing this candidate always provides the largest profit for the group.

Shown in Figure 14, the baseline model examines how participants' own motivations influence their propensity to vote correctly based on their individualistic utility. By this definition, participants in the control condition have a .73 probability of voting correctly, assuming they have the median level of expertise. Consistent with *correct voting hypothesis 1*, participants with prosocial motivations vote correctly at a greater rate, with a .78 probability (first difference = .05, p = .02).

A similar pattern emerges when controlling for informants' motivations. And when further examining informants' motivations, we see that participants whose informants had prosocial motivations were significantly more likely to vote correctly than those who did not receive social information. This result is consistent with the *prosocial informant hypothesis*, but this relationship may not be causal, since participants' decision to seek information was not randomly assigned.

Figure 15 plots an analogous model where the dependent variable is again correct voting, but this time a correct vote is classified as cases where the participant selected the candidate most proximate to the median voter. Here we see that prosocial motivations helped participants vote not only in their own interest, but also in the best interest of the group – as *correct voting hypothesis 2* predicted. Participants with prosocial motivations voted for the group's

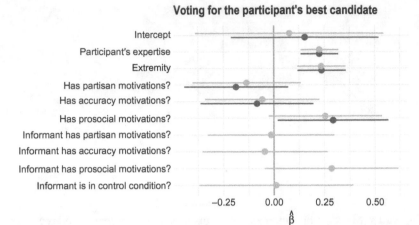

Figure 14 Results from a logistic regression show that participants with elevated prosocial motivations are more likely to vote correctly.

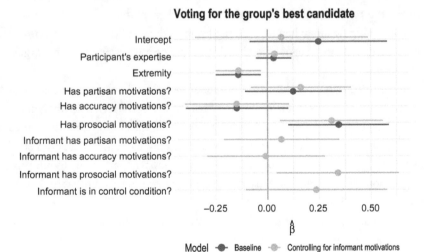

Figure 15 Results from a logistic regression show that participants with elevated prosocial motivations are more likely to support the best candidate for the group.

optimal candidate about 60 percent of the time, while participants in the control condition did so only about half the time (first difference = .602 − .516 = .09, p < .01).

When controlling for informants' motivations, participants whose informants held prosocial motivations were *not* significantly more collectivist in their voting than participants whose informants were in the control condition. They were, however, significantly more collectivist than those who did not seek social information (first difference = .56 − .47 = .09, p = .01). Together, Figures 14 and 15 suggest that prosocial motivations help individuals pursue their own interests while also encouraging them to choose the best candidate for the group as a whole. However, the results about the effect of informants' motivations rest on weaker evidence. Since the choice of informant is not randomly assigned, inclusion of controls constitutes a form of posttreatment bias. Further, it creates a number of potentially relevant comparisons, only some of which are consistent with our expectations − a common problem for experiments in the behavioral economics tradition. We expand on this point in the next and final section.

4.6 Conclusion

The results from this section demonstrate that the nature and effectiveness of political communication depend on the motivations of both the individual and their informant. Participants in the control condition replicated the results from previous research. They sought information from experts whose positions were close to their own. They sent messages that increased in bias as their position diverged from the recipient's position. And they often failed to benefit from communication, unless they held little private information. Prosocial-motivated participants differed markedly from those in the control condition, however. They sent less biased messages − particularly when informing ideologically distant participants − and they voted correctly at a greater rate − both for their own best candidate and for the group's best candidate. Thus, while prosocial motivations emphasize others' well-being, they also help individuals pursue their own well-being.

Just like in Section 3, our results here provide methodological insight about using small-group experiments to study elections. They provide substantive insight about how motivations affect political judgments, the efficacy of political discussion, and the conditions that can promote deliberative democratic ideals. Methodologically, they demonstrate that participants' behavior in small-group election experiments are sensitive to small changes in incentives. The experiment presented here mimics the common structure of the election-style experiments that are increasingly used to study political discussion. Unlike many of these designs, however, this one varied incentives within groups and between participants, providing an opportunity to examine how incentives influence the conclusions one might draw about the nature and effectiveness of political communication.

Looking only at participants in the control condition, one would conclude that communication tends to be strategic, self-interested, and occasionally self-defeating. Looking at participants with prosocial motivations, however, one would conclude communication can be mutually beneficial, if still strategic. These differences in behavior arising from small differences in incentives suggest future work take care aligning experimental incentives with the motivations elicited in the real-world contexts of interest. Conversely, participants with stronger partisan motivations behaved much like those in the control condition. Since the control mimics previous experiments, the absence of meaningful differences suggests past work baked partisan motivations in from the start – as we discussed in Section 2.

Substantively, our results demonstrate that communication is not inherently strategic nor prosocial, but rather its efficacy depends on discussants' motivations. Contrary to much of the experimental discussion literature, these results suggest informal communication *can* promote deliberative ideals. When participants had incentives to care about their recipients' well-being, they were more helpful in their communication, but also performed better themselves. In this context, self-interest does not necessarily conflict with the common good – by helping others, people can also help themselves. At the same time, the results reinforce an emerging theme from Ahn and colleagues' recent work: when participants are motivated by strategic ends, the effectiveness of communication is muted. By ignoring the role of motivations, the literature has implicitly focused only on these more strategic interactions, overlooking important heterogeneity in the effects of communication. By delineating the role of motivations, our results can provide guidance for how discussion may function in other contexts, societies, or cultures where levels of altruism are likely to differ.

The findings in this section also contribute to the political science literature on motivated reasoning by exploring judgment in social, rather than isolated, settings and under a wider spectrum of motivations than previous studies. As Klar (2014; 688) notes, most political science research focuses on the motivations of individuals acting in isolation, but social settings can produce markedly different results. Klar (2014) demonstrates that particular forms of discussion can promote or inhibit particular motivations – people in more heterogeneous social groups exhibit less partisan-motivated reasoning. The analysis here demonstrates the reciprocal relationship: particular motivations cause particular forms of discussion. By exploring prosocial motivations, this experiment also examines a broader range of motivations than most political science work, which often focuses only on partisan motivations.[24]

---

[24] Indeed, political scientists often conflate the term "motivated reasoning" with partisan-motivated reasoning, in contradiction to the belief common among psychologists that information processing is always motivated, at least in part, to achieve accuracy (see Kruglanski & Boyatzi, 2012; 219–223).

Druckman (2012) argues that the discipline's focus on partisan motivations has underestimated citizens' democratic competence. The results here suggest prosocial motivations – long a focus of deliberative theorists – can indeed promote democratic competence, improving individuals' ability to foster outcomes better for themselves and the group as a whole. Of course, prosocial motivations are unlikely to be effective in all contexts. Even accuracy motivations can fail to promote better judgments (Pietryka, 2016). Thus, future work must explore how these motivations operate in other settings, judgments, and decisions.

The results in this section seem to contradict previous work because they demonstrate the potential for political discussion to lead to aggregate enlightenment. There are a couple of possible reasons for this and they both relate to aspects of design we have stressed in this Element. The obvious reason is related to incentives. In this experiment, unlike in the previous experiments, senders' payoffs depended on receivers making decisions that were best for the receivers and not necessarily the senders. This reduces the incentive for participants to mislead others.

We have also noted that a key design aspect that is too often ignored is experimental instructions. Instructions can signal to participants that the researchers expect them to behave in a particular manner, altering their behavior and serving essentially as an implicit "treatment" (in some cases, assigned to every participant). In this experiment, the instructions in the prosocial treatment shift the focus away from the individual participant and onto *all* participants. This should augment the effect of financial incentives, as it suggests participants should not simply focus on maximizing their own payoffs.

Consider this in the context of a group-based study with very different characteristics than the ones we have discussed to this point: the deliberative poll of Fishkin and colleagues (2021). The authors show that deliberation can depolarize citizen attitudes. They emphasize the importance of shifting people away from directional goals and toward accuracy goals when processing information. We imagine, however, that this is less important than the efforts the researchers took to ensure that every individual in a deliberative group is seen as equal to everyone else. People felt less of a need to defend their partisan positions when the group was more important than any individual participant. In group-based experiments, the treatments and instructions set expectations about the relationships between the participants. The designs in this section's experiment and in Fishkin and colleagues (2021) set different expectations than the previous experiments we have discussed. And, as a result, they lead to different conclusions about the potential for interpersonal communication.

5 Advice on Experimental Design

In this final section, we use our two experiments to illuminate factors that we hope scholars consider when designing and analyzing their own small-group experiments. We want to note two things about the discussion in this section. First, this advice applies to these group-based, incentivized experiments generally and not only to those looking at motivations. Second, the approach we used throughout this Element is not the only way to approach the study of motivations in discussion. For instance, Carlson (2021) uses a variety of creative survey experiments to examine how political communication changes when individuals are motivated to seek political information rather than acquiring information casually. In one experiment, subjects communicate over multiple, asynchronous stages – rather than in a single synchronous session like our subjects participate in. In her studies, the subjects in subsequent stages are assigned to read messages sent in a previous stage, avoiding interdependence that can be a nuisance for inference. Yet the designs we use here have many advantages, as we have described throughout this Element. Therefore, we offer several suggestions for working with similar incentivized, group experiments.

To help scholars build upon our experimental framework, we have created a set of materials, including z-Tree treatment and questionnaire files, code for reading in z-Tree data in Stata and R, and complete replication materials of the analysis presented in this Element. Those files are available at the Harvard Dataverse repository. Finally, we have assembled checklists we use when planning and fielding experiments like these, which can be found in the Supporting Information (SI-C).

Again, these designs provide useful insight into complex, interdependent processes by stripping away extraneous and confounding elements. Yet these benefits also come with important trade-offs that scholars should be aware of before deciding to pursue similar designs. Perhaps most importantly, stripping away extraneous and confounding elements creates threats to a design's external validity. In this section, we discuss several considerations we use to address this challenge.

In addition to external validity limitations, small-group experiments feature several challenges that are absent from most experiments where subjects participate independently from one another. In particular, we discuss the challenges in analyzing interdependent observations, how interdependence influences statistical power, and how to avoid posttreatment bias when dependent variables are gathered at several stages of a dynamic interaction.

5.1 External Validity

To isolate the effects of motivations and communication, the previous sections' research designs abstract away from real-world elections. To vote in our experimental elections, participants do not need to wait in line at their polling places; they do not need to navigate the bureaucracy to register to vote or obtain an absentee ballot; they are never inundated by messages from campaign mailers, radio talk show hosts, or social media acquaintances. They are never distracted by the banalities, joys, and tragedies that permeate day-to-day living – aside from those occurring in their lives on the day of the study (Druckman & Leeper, 2012).

By removing these elements, we are not denying their importance in real-world elections. Rather, we sacrifice these important considerations in our experimental setting so we can better examine several other features of real-world elections that are difficult to examine with observational data. Unlike observational studies, which have difficulty determining when discussion leads to opinion change (Fowler et al., 2011), these experiments measure beliefs *as* they develop, isolating the effect of information. Since we have measures of each participant's beliefs *and* the messages they send, we can also objectively measure the sincerity of subjects' communications – a notoriously difficult concept to measure (Neblo, 2015; 35). Likewise, the designs provide straight-forward, unambiguous measures of the quality of subjects' beliefs and vote choices. Last, observational studies – while potentially more externally valid – cannot determine conclusively which motivations individuals possess. For this reason, Leeper and Slothuus (2014; 149) contend, "experiments where motivations are primed are the best – and perhaps only – way to clearly distinguish the effects and mechanisms of motivated reasoning."

Yet all research requires trade-offs, and these advantages require many abstractions from reality. Therefore, it is essential to consider how these abstractions might influence the generalizability of our results. In particular, how does the absence of these elements influence the generalizability of our conclusions? One obvious threat to external validity is our use of student samples. Student samples receive frequent criticism because students' attitudes differ in both character and malleability from those of other adults (Krupnikov & Levine, 2014; Sears, 1986). In contrast to most laboratory experiments, however, our designs limit this threat by *assigning* positions and expertise rather than relying on students' preexisting attitudes or knowledge.

Brutger and colleagues (2020) provide a threefold framework for evaluating how a design's level of realism or abstraction might influence results.

Their framework asks researchers to classify an experiment on three dimensions, which they label situational hypothetically, actor identity, and contextual detail. *Situational hypothetically* reflects whether subjects knew they were evaluating a hypothetical rather than real scenario. On this dimension, our experiments skew away from abstraction since participants know that their choices have real, specific consequences. *Actor identity* reflects whether the focal actors in the experiment are real or fictional. Though the subjects knew the voters were real people, they also knew the task was to elect a fictional candidate. The artificial nature of these candidates – represented only by a numeric position and a generic label (Candidate A or Candidate B) – places our experiments far on the abstract side of the dimension. The final dimension, *contextual detail*, reflects how rich and detailed the experimental scenario is for subjects. Here, our experiments also fall far on the abstract side of this dimension since they make no effort to mimic real-world voting scenarios. Indeed, our goal was to remove all but the most essential elements of an election.

In general, though, Brutger and colleagues (2020) find that none of these dimensions have large, predictable implications for the experimental results. In particular, they find little evidence of variation in effects based on situational hypothetically. Likewise, they find only small variation in effect sizes due to actor identity. The exception is that well-known candidates – as compared to fictional candidates – can have larger effects when endorsing policies. We note, however, that by stripping away party labels, we remove a key determinant of voting in real-world elections. We make this choice deliberately since real-world partisanship itself is endogenous to expertise, extremity, and psychological motivations. With party labels, our small incentives may not have been strong enough to generate the motivations we sought to study. Ultimately, then, whether this sacrifice was worthwhile depends on whether we succeeded in generating the motivations of interest. Therefore, the incentive structure in our experiments deserves additional scrutiny.

5.1.1 Getting the Incentives Right

When designing incentivized experiments, the incentives themselves require great scrutiny. Many pages have been written debating incentive structures, and thus we cannot do this literature justice in this short Element – for several thoughtful reviews, see Dickson (2011); Fehr, Goette, and Zehnder (2009); and Kamenica (2012). The decision regarding incentives is especially delicate since one must choose these *prior* to fielding the study, but readers' assessment of the "correct" incentives are typically formed only after the results are in. Thus, readers exhibiting hindsight bias (Roese & Vohs, 2012) may argue that any null results stem from insufficient incentives, while any observed effects may be artifacts of the incentive structure – "well, sure, if you pay people to do that, they will."

Both of these criticisms merit attention in our studies. Some readers may worry that the incentives are so large that they ensure subjects behave in specific ways. Yet all of our treatments provide small incentives relative to the overriding incentive to elect the candidate closest to one's own position. For instance, in Section 4 (and previous research on the topic) electing the closest candidate produces a one-dollar swing in a subject's fortune. By contrast, subjects gain only an extra quarter if they help a fellow subject vote correctly in the prosocial treatment. And thus, *all* subjects are better off electing the best candidate for themselves. These relatively small incentives should bias results toward the null, providing a conservative test for the effects of motivations.[25]

But if these incentives are small, readers may worry that the incentives are insufficient to induce the motivations of interest. While ideally the experiment's prosocial motivations would encourage the trust and affection many people feel toward their real-world discussants, this design must create prosocial motivations instrumentally. Nonetheless, motivations to promote the well-being of others arise when subjects' outcomes are tied to the success of other subjects (Weingart, Bennett, & Brett, 1993). And as we show in the previous sections, important differences in behavior emerge *despite* these relatively small differences in incentives.

Since these criticisms are valid and unavoidable, we believe they should be addressed in two ways. First, researchers should scale the incentives in proportion to the theoretical incentives of interest. In our case, working within the Downsian framework, we sought to ensure that each participant's primary incentive was electing the most proximate candidate. We then added small incentives to examine how motivations change behavior *despite* the powerful incentive to act in a self-interested way.

Second, researchers should examine the extent to which the incentives generated the psychological and behavioral processes of interest. For example, in the experiment described in Section 4, we examined whether our accuracy and directional treatments caused participants to process information in a manner consistent with how people process information with real-world accuracy and directional motivations. Accuracy motivations are typified by greater investment in the search for information and greater effort in processing the information (Kunda, 1990). Thus, subjects with accuracy incentives should be

---

[25] The prosocial treatment, in particular, is an especially conservative test, given that an extra quarter in the experiment represents the strength of real human connection with both strangers and close friends and family.

more likely to request social information and spend more time evaluating the social information they receive. We observed both patterns: 91 percent of subjects with accuracy motivations requested social information – compared to 85 percent of subjects without these motivations ($\chi^2_{df=1} = 10.1; p = .001$) – and subjects with accuracy motivations also spent about 1.5 seconds longer, on average, on the screen in which they received social information and entered their candidate judgments.[26]

Partisan motivations drive people to read beyond the available information, increasing the chances they come to a predetermined conclusion. Therefore, if the partisan incentives worked, participants in the partisan treatment should be more likely than the others to support their candidate – even after controlling for the information they received about the candidate positions. This pattern occurs as expected, as shown in Table 1. The table shows three logistic regressions in which the dependent variable indicates whether the participant voted for Candidate A or B in an election. In Model 1, the only independent variables are indicators of whether the participant was assigned to the Party A partisan treatment or the Party B partisan treatment. The positive coefficient associated with Party A indicates that these subjects were more likely to support Candidate A than participants not in the partisan treatment. Likewise, the negative coefficient associated with Party B indicates that Party B partisans were less likely to support Candidate A (and thus more likely to support Candidate B) than were participants not in the partisan treatment. Therefore, both groups of partisans supported their candidate at greater rates than subjects who were not in either partisan treatment.

Model 2 demonstrates that this pattern persists after controlling for the information that each participant received about the candidates. Finally, Model 3 examines the possibility that partisan voting is used only as a response to uncertainty. Recall that in the experiments, subjects are always better off if the most proximate candidate wins, regardless of whether they hold partisan motivations. Thus, if they are certain that one candidate is more proximate than the other, they should always vote for that candidate – their partisan incentives should have no effect. If subjects are rational and self-interested,

---

[26] This analysis is based on only five of the six sessions. In the sixth session, the z-Tree experimental software did not record response times because the laboratory computers had been running for more than twenty-four hours, precluding accurate response-time measurement. Using response times to study depth of processing requires careful consideration of the response time distribution, which often features long right tails. To prevent outliers from having undue influence over the regression estimates, researchers often log the response time or instead model the rank order of the response (e.g., Petersen et al., 2013). Either approach yields a statistically significant beta in the regression of response time on whether the participant is in the accuracy treatment.

Table 1 Participants' vote choice by whether they were assigned to the partisan treatment

	Model 1	Model 2	Model 3
Has Party A partisan motivations?	0.63*	0.83*	0.65*
(0 = No; 1 = Yes)	(0.13)	(0.16)	(0.27)
Has Party B partisan motivations?	−0.36*	−0.73*	−1.02*
(0 = No; 1 = Yes)	(0.13)	(0.16)	(0.27)
A's advantage based on private		0.43*	0.43*
information		(0.03)	(0.03)
A's advantage based on social		0.52*	0.52*
information		(0.03)	(0.03)
Certainty (|Perceived Relative			−0.18*
Proximity|)			(0.07)
Has Party A Partisan Motivations?			0.12
× Certainty			(0.15)
Has Party B Partisan Motivations?			0.19
× Certainty			(0.14)
Intercept	0.10	0.09	0.36*
	(0.07)	(0.08)	(0.14)
N - Observations	1,890	1,890	1,890
N - Participants	126	126	126
N - Elections	15	15	15
Variance(Intercept) - Participants	0.10	0.18	0.19
Variance(Intercept) - Elections	0.00	0.00	0.00
Log Likelihood	−1,282.95	−950.85	−947.37
AIC	2,575.91	1,915.70	1,914.75

$^*p < 0.05$

Note: Reported coefficients are from multilevel logistic regressions (with standard errors in parentheses). Observations represent participants in an election. Intercepts vary across elections and unique participants. The dependent variable equals one if the subject voted for Candidate A and zero if the subject voted for Candidate B. Certainty is measured as the absolute value of the subject's perceived relative proximity to Candidate A (where perceived relative proximity is measured as the absolute difference between the subject's judgment of Candidate B's position and the subject's own position, minus the absolute difference between the subject's judgment of Candidate A's position and the subject's own position).

partisan incentives should only affect voting for subjects who are *uncertain* about which candidate is most proximate.[27]

As Model 3 shows, however, the effect of partisan motivations does not attenuate significantly with increases in participants' certainty. When subjects place the candidates at the same position – and thus are maximally uncertain about which candidate is most proximate (i.e., Certainty = 0) – Party A motivations are expected to double the odds of voting for Candidate A.[28] When subjects place one candidate a unit more proximate than the opponent (i.e., Certainty = 1) – and are therefore slightly more certain – the odds ratio associated with Party A motivations increases to 2.2, but this increase is not statistically significant.[29] Thus, the Party A motivations pull individuals toward their party's candidate and, at times, away from supporting the most proximate candidate. Party B motivations have a similar effect in the opposite direction. The main effect is negative and statistically significant. While the marginal effect does attenuate in magnitude with increases in certainty, this interaction lacks statistical significance. Thus, certainty does not systematically attenuate the effects and therefore, much like in the real world, partisan motivations occasionally undermine individuals' ability to pursue their own best interests.

5.2 The Challenges of Interdependence

Network experiments such as these are designed to examine interdependence, but therefore require analysis that accounts for this interdependence. In a simple survey experiment, a researcher typically randomizes participants into either treatment or control. They then measure the difference in the average responses in the treatment to those in the control, inferring that this difference is due to the effect of the treatment itself rather than any alternative explanations. This inference requires the assumption that one participant's response is not influenced by whether any other participant was assigned to the treatment or control.[30] If this assumption is violated, the researcher may over- or underestimate the treatment effect. The interdependence is also a problem at the modeling phase since regression models require the assumption that the errors are independent. Thus, when this assumption is violated, the betas may be incorrect and standard errors biased toward zero.

---

[27] Specifically, partisan incentives should affect an individual's vote choice only if $.35 < p < .5$, where p is their subjective probability that their party's candidate is most proximate.

[28] $\exp(\beta_{\text{Has Party A Partisan Motivations?}}) = \exp(0.68) = 2.0$

[29] $\exp(\beta_{\text{Has Party A Partisan Motivations?}} + \beta_{\text{Has Party A Partisan Motivations?}}) = \exp(0.68 + .12) = 2.2$

[30] An assumption formally called the Stable Unit Treatment Value Assumption and abbreviated as *SUTVA*.

5.2.1 The Source of Interdependence

In studies like ours where participants can communicate, these assumptions are unlikely to hold. In our designs, interdependence can arise from several sources. First, interdependence can arise between individuals within elections. Most obviously, this pattern arises when participants communicate with one another. But this interdependence can also occur due to election-level variables that influence multiple participants at once – for instance, the positions of the candidates may influence many participants since they are responding to the same candidates. Second, interdependence can arise *within* individuals between elections. Since each participant takes part in many different elections, they may rely on similar strategies from one election to the next – for example, a participant who tends to be more cooperative than others is likely to conduct themselves in a cooperative manner throughout each election.

5.2.2 Accounting for Interdependence

We take a threefold path to account for interdependence. First, we seek to avoid model bias by explicitly modeling the the sources of interdependence (Kenny & Judd, 1986). Second, we limit the opportunities for communication to those we can observe and measure. Third, we check our assumptions against the data to evaluate the need for additional correction.

To model the interdependence, we rely on multilevel models, which can account for interdependence by using varying intercepts to account for group-level differences. Multilevel models were originally developed in education research to examine student-level outcomes. Since students are nested within classrooms and classrooms are nested within schools, one student's performance will be systematically linked to the performance of other students in the same class and school. Multilevel models provide a means to relax the independence assumption by specifying the groups where interdependence may occur. By allowing the intercept to vary across groups, these models separate group-level variation from individual-level variation. For this reason, textbooks often recommend multilevel models for network data (Crossley et al., 2015; Snijders & Bosker, 2012). In our case, we estimate models with intercepts that vary (1) across elections to account for interdependence between individuals within elections and (2) across *participants* to account for interdependence within individuals *between* elections.

Interdependence can only be modeled if its sources can readily be measured. Therefore, great care must be taken when designing and conducting group-level experiments like ours. Indeed, a chief advantage of these abstract experiments is that they provide a simple way to structure and measure the communication.

Within an election, we observe who communicates with whom, who initiates the communication, and what they say. Yet this approach works only if we also prevent communication by other means during the experiment. If two participants sat next to each other and shared information verbally during the study, we could not measure this communication and therefore could not account for it in our models. To avoid this problem, we seat people who arrive together in different parts of the laboratory and program the computer terminals so that direct neighbors are not in the same experimental group. Likewise, we do not allow talking or mobile devices during a session.

Despite these precautions, we can never be sure we have modeled or avoided all sources of interdependence. Therefore, we always examine our data to check our assumptions. A properly specified multilevel model should address the dependence in the data and thus the residuals should not exhibit any remaining correlation with adjacent units. Moran's I statistic, developed for spatial econometrics, provides a test of this assumption. Generally speaking, Moran's I measures how strongly individual observations of a variable are associated with the observations of other proximate individuals in the data. To estimate this statistic, one must specify the variable to examine and a metric on which to measure proximity. Here, the variable of interest is the model residuals. In many applications, this proximity measure may be physical space such as an indicator of whether pairs of countries share a border. In social networks, this proximity measure typically represents an indicator of whether pairs of individuals share a link in the network (Anselin, 2010).

Much like a correlation coefficient, Moran's I varies from -1 to 1 with values further from 0 indicating stronger interdependence and the sign indicating the direction of association. Thus, we typically expect a positive association if interdependence remains. Values close to 0 indicate little remaining interdependence. We use a Monte Carlo approach to assess the statistical significance of the estimate, randomly permuting the proximity variable and then calculating a new Moran's I statistic. We repeat this process a thousand times, yielding a distribution of Moran's I statistics we would expect to observe by chance. This approach provides a p-value that represents the proportion of permutations in which the Moran's I statistic is greater for the randomly assigned values than in the observed data. As an example, Table 2 shows the Moran's I statistics for each model presented in Section 4. For the estimates in the table, we examine interdependence between participants within elections.[31]

---

[31] We have also estimated this for interdependence within participants between elections, but find little evidence of remaining interdependence at this level. We therefore present the election-level statistics to focus attention on instances that might require corrective action.

Table 2 Moran's I statistics for the models reported in Section 4

Moran's I	p-value	Figure	Dependant Variable
−0.002	0.999	11	Information request
−0.008	0.998	13	Message bias
−0.008	0.996	13	Message bias
0.005	0.074	14	Correct voting - Self interest
0.006	0.069	14	Correct voting - Self interest
0.001	0.316	15	Correct voting - Group interest
0.000	0.396	15	Correct voting - Group interest

In the table, the Moran's I statistics are all near zero, indicating no apparent interdependence in the residuals at the election level. Though substantively small, two Moran's I statistics produce p-values less than 0.1. In such cases, we turn to spatial econometric models to account for the remaining interdependence. The most commonly used spatial regression model among political scientists is the spatial lag (Ward & Gleditsch, 2008; 69). Indeed, several studies have used this model to examine political discussion (Makse, Minkoff, & Sokhey, 2019, 2014; Pietryka et al., 2018). The spatial lag model can be expressed as $Y = \rho \mathbf{W}y + \mathbf{X}\beta + \epsilon$. Like classic regression, the outcome Y is a function of exogenous covariates $\mathbf{X}$ plus an error term. Unlike classic regression, the outcome also depends on a spatial lag $\mathbf{W}y$, where $\mathbf{W}$ is an $n \times n$ matrix in which the entry in the ith row and j^{th} column specifies the proximity of observation i to observation j. In the model, ρ thus represents the level of dependence between connected observations. This model controls for this interdependence when estimating the remaining slope coefficients and their standard errors.

Table 3 shows the spatial lag regressions of correct voting. In both models, ρ is positive and statistically significant, indicating the presence of interdependence between participants within elections. Yet the other coefficients and standard errors remain almost identical to the original estimates from the multilevel model as shown in Figure 14. We also subject each of these new model's residuals to another Moran's I test, displayed at the bottom of the table. The Moran's I from each model's residuals remains substantively small (.002 and .001) and the p-values are larger (.24 and .27) than those from the multilevel models.

Rather than modeling interdependence, however, researchers may instead seek to *reduce* interdependence by changing the unit of analysis from individuals to groups. For instance, in Section 3, the expertise and communication gap treatments were assigned at the group level. In Figures 8 and 9, we examined

Table 3 Linear spatial lag regressions of correct voting based on self-interest. The standard errors are adjusted using White's heteroskedasticity-consistent correction.

	Model 1	Model 2
Extremity (|Position − Median Position|)	0.043*	0.043*
	(0.011)	(0.011)
Subject's expertise (Number of pieces of private information)	0.045*	0.045*
	(0.008)	(0.009)
Has partisan motivations?	−0.034	−0.025
(0 = No; 1 = Yes)	(0.024)	(0.025)
Has accuracy motivations?	−0.021	−0.015
(0 = No; 1 = Yes)	(0.025)	(0.025)
Has prosocial motivations?	0.047*	0.041
(0 = No; 1 = Yes)	(0.024)	(0.024)
S's informant has partisan motivations?		−0.002
(0 = No; 1 = Yes)		(0.028)
S's informant has accuracy motivations?		−0.016
(0 = No; 1 = Yes)		(0.028)
S's informant has prosocial motivations?		0.051
(0 = No; 1 = Yes)		(0.028)
S's informant is in control condition?		−0.010
(0 = No; 1 = Yes)		(0.034)
ρ (Spatial Dependence)	0.956*	0.950*
	(0.195)	(0.148)
Intercept	−0.131	−0.136
	(0.143)	(0.112)
N	1,558	1,558
Moran's I	0.002	0.001
Moran's I p-value	0.260	0.272

*$p < 0.05$

how these treatments influence the vote margin for the candidate who provides the greatest benefit to the group's welfare. In this analysis, we need only to model the interdependence of each group's behavior from one election to the next, since no dependence is feasible between different groups. Yet this approach is only useful when researchers do not wish to examine variation in treatment effects among individuals. For instance, in Figures 3 - 7 of the same section, we examined how these treatments impact extremists and moderates in distinct ways. In these cases, therefore, we must still account for the potential of within-group interdependence. Also, shifting from individual-level analysis to group-level analysis requires more observations to achieve sufficient statistical power.

5.3 Maximizing Statistical Power

Interdependence not only makes the analysis more complicated than typical survey experiments, it also requires larger samples in order to obtain sufficient statistical power (Sinclair, McConnell, & Green, 2012). To address this challenge, researchers may choose to increase the number of observations by increasing the number of people who participate in the study or the number of rounds that each person participates in. In our experience, it is typically more efficient to increase the number of rounds than it is to increase the total number of participants. This choice saves time because it requires fewer training sessions. It also saves money because the total cost of the experiment depends on the show-up fee paid to all people who arrive at the laboratory plus the individual incentives earned each round. By adding rounds rather than participants, one can increase statistical power without paying additional show-up fees. Moreover, to ensure a session runs, a researcher typically must recruit more participants than needed and thus must pay additional show-up fees to people who do not participate. Thus, adding more participants requires more sessions, more money spent, and a higher proportion of money spent on nonparticipants.

Yet adding more rounds creates costs too. One large challenge is that participants' behavior may change over the duration of the session, perhaps due to boredom or learning. Regardless of the cause, this change can create an additional source of interdependence if participants tend to systematically change in similar ways. Researchers often evaluate this threat by examining the earlier and later rounds separately to ensure they produce similar results, but examining the correlation of residuals as described in the previous section is a more systematic test of this threat. Adding more rounds rather than participants may also limit the diversity of the sample. Though laboratory studies typically lack representative samples, they can overcome this by modeling expected heterogeneity in treatment effects (Druckman & Kam, 2012). Yet this feat is only possible if the sample provides sufficient variation on theoretically relevant sources of heterogeneity.

5.4 Avoiding Posttreatment Bias

Our last piece of advice is on how to avoid post treatment bias. Our designs allow us to observe every stage of interpersonal communication – with whom one communicates, what they communicate, and how that communication influences subsequent judgments and behavior. Yet this wealth presents a new source of bias that may be easy to overlook. Consider the analysis summarized in Figure 12. In the plot, the baseline model shows the average message bias based on each participant's motivations. A second model in the plot estimates how the average bias changes with the distance between the sender and receiver. Including distance as an independent variable changes the interpretation of the coefficients associated with each set of motivations. These coefficients no longer represent treatment effects because distance is caused by assignment to treatment – thus its inclusion in the model removes one mechanism by which the treatments influence message bias.[32]

To avoid this bias entirely, one could restrict analysis only to randomly assigned variables. In most settings, this recommendation is reasonable and well justified (Montgomery, Nyhan, & Torres, 2018). At best, models conditioning on post treatment variables constitute observational analyses, which often require heroic assumptions to interpret as causal. But a chief advantage of our designs is that they remove many of the confounds present in real-world communication, requiring less stringent identifying assumptions. Thus the observational results may still be worth exploring as a means of process tracing, even if they require stronger identifying assumptions for inference than analysis of the randomly assigned variables. In these cases, we strive to clarify which estimates can be interpreted as causal, flag those that require stronger assumptions, and justify the examination of such quantities despite their lack of experimental identification. Without great care, readers may otherwise mistake such estimates as causal since they come from an experimental research design.

5.5 Try This at Home!

This section listed a number of potential difficulties in the design and analysis of experiments of this type. We did not discuss the difficulties in actually running the experiments – for example, we had to use a computer classroom when we first ran experiments of this type more than fifteen years ago because we did not have access to an experimental laboratory. And, certainly, these types of studies are costly both in terms of time and money. They can also be difficult to publish because they differ from the standard studies reviewers who study elections and voting typically see and run themselves.

That all being said, we wrote this section with the hope that it will provide researchers with information they need to run studies of this type on

---

[32] The interactive nature of the model also means these coefficients cannot be interpreted as average treatment effects because they represent estimates for dyads where distance equals zero.

their own. We see these studies as building on our previous work as well as hopefully illuminating more about the motivations driving people when they engage in interpersonal communication and the consequences *of* those motivations. At the same time, since the studies published here are based on previous studies *we* did before (some with other coauthors), they are not a large departure from what came before. We look forward to reading work from different scholars illuminating elements of interpersonal communications that we never considered.

References

Ahn, T. K., Huckfeldt, R., Mayer, A. K., & Ryan, J. B. (2013, April). Expertise and Bias in Political Communication Networks. *American Journal of Political Science, 57*(2), 357–373. https://doi.org/10.1111/j.1540-5907.2012.00625.x.

Ahn, T. K., Huckfeldt, R., & Ryan, J. B. (2010). Communication, Influence, and Informational Asymmetries among Voters. *Political Psychology, 31*(5), 763–787.

Ahn, T. K., Huckfeldt, R., & Ryan, J. B. (2014). *Experts, Activists, and Interdependent Citizens: Are Electorates Self-Educating?* New York: Cambridge University Press.

Ahn, T. K., & Ryan, J. B. (2015, July). The Overvaluing of Expertise in Discussion Partner Choice. *Journal of Theoretical Politics, 27*(3), 380–400. http://jtp.sagepub.com/content/27/3/380. https://doi.org/10.1177/0951629814531672.

Anselin, L. (2010, March). Thirty Years of Spatial Econometrics. *Papers in Regional Science, 89*(1), 3–25. https://doi.org/10.1111/j.1435-5957.2010.00279.x.

Bafumi, J., & Herron, M. C. (2010). Leapfrog Representation and Extremism: A Study of American Voters and Their Members in Congress. *American Political Science Review, 104*(3), 519–542. https://doi.org/10.1017/S0003055410000316.

Bail, C. A., Argyle, L. P., Brown, T. W., et al. (2018, September). Exposure to Opposing Views on Social Media Can Increase Political Polarization. *Proceedings of the National Academy of Sciences, 115*(37), 9216–9221. www.pnas.org/content/115/37/9216. https://doi.org/10.1073/pnas.1804840115.

Barabas, J. (2004). How Deliberation Affects Policy Opinions. *American Political Science Review, 98*(4), 687–701. https://doi.org/10.1017/S0003055404041425

Baron, D. P. (1994). Electoral Competition with Informed and Uninformed Voters. *American Political Science Review, 88*(1), 33–47. www.jstor.org/stable/2944880.

Batson, C. D. (2016, October). Empathy and Altruism. In K. W. Brown & M. R. Leary (eds.), *The Oxford Handbook of Hypo-egoic Phenomena* (pp. 161–174). New York: Oxford University Press.

Batson, C. D., Ahmad, N., Powell, A. A., & Stocks, E. L. (2008). Prosocial Motivation. In J. Y. Shah & W. L. Gardner (eds.), *Handbook of Motivation Science* (pp. 135–149). New York: Guilford.

Batson, C. D., & Shaw, L. L. (1991). Evidence for Altruism: Toward a Pluralism of Prosocial Motives. *Psychological Inquiry, 2*(2), 107–122. www.jstor.org/stable/1449242.

Baumeister, R. F., & Newman, L. S. (1994, February). Self-Regulation of Cognitive Inference and Decision Processes. *Personality and Social Psychology Bulletin, 20*(1), 3–19. https://doi.org/10.1177/0146167294201001.

Bayes, R., Druckman, J. N., Goods, A., & Molden, D. C. (2020, October). When and How Different Motives Can Drive Motivated Political Reasoning. *Political Psychology, 41*(5), 1031–1052. https://doi.org/10.1111/pops.12663.

Bond, R. M., Fariss, C. J., Jones, J. J., et al. (2012, September). A 61-Million-Person Experiment in Social Influence and Political Mobilization. *Nature, 489*(7415), 295–298. https://doi.org/10.1038/nature11421.

Brutger, R., Kertzer, J. D., Renshon, J., Tingley, D., & Weiss, C. M. (2020, September). Abstraction and Detail in Experimental Design. https://people.fas.harvard.edu/~jkertzer/Research_files/AbstractConcrete%20091620_Website.pdf.

Budge, I. (1994, October). A New Spatial Theory of Party Competition: Uncertainty, Ideology and Policy Equilibria Viewed Comparatively and Temporally. *British Journal of Political Science, 24*(4), 443–467. www.cambridge.org/core/journals/british-journal-of-political-science/article/abs/new-spatial-theory-of-party-competition-uncertainty-ideology-and-policy-equilibria-viewed-comparatively-and-temporally/85720AA3AF1595792CE6BD95E79C38E9. https://doi.org/10.1017/S0007123400006955.

Calvert, R. L. (1985, June). The Value of Biased Information: A Rational Choice Model of Political Advice. *Journal of Politics, 47*(2), 530–555. https://doi.org/10.2307/2130895.

Carlson, T. N. (2018). Modeling Political Information Transmission As a Game of Telephone. *Journal of Politics, 80*(1), 348–352. https://doi.org/10.1086/694767.

Carlson, T. N. (2019, May). Through the Grapevine: Informational Consequences of Interpersonal Political Communication. *American Political Science Review, 113*(2), 325–339. www.cambridge.org/core/journals/american-political-science-review/article/through-the-grapevine-informational-consequences-of-interpersonal-political-communication/6CBBDCAD4AF791DA8C446F9B502FDD90/core-reader. https://doi.org/10.1017/S000305541900008X.

Carlson, T. N. (2021, October 29). *Through the Grapevine: Political Conversations and Distorted Democracy.*

Carlson, T. N., & Settle, J. E. (2016, December). Political Chameleons: An Exploration of Conformity in Political Discussions. *Political Behavior, 38*(4), 817–859. https://doi.org/10.1007/s11109-016-9335-y.

Carlson, T. N., & Settle, J. E. (2022). *What Goes Without Saying: Navigating Political Discussion in America.* New York: Cambridge University Press.

Connors, E. C., Krupnikov, Y., & Ryan, J. B. (2019, July). How Transparency Affects Survey Responses. *Public Opinion Quarterly, 83*(S1), 185–209. https://academic.oup.com/poq/article/83/S1/185/5520299. https://doi.org/10.1093/poq/nfz013.

Conover, P. J., Searing, D. D., & Crewe, I. M. (2002, January). The Deliberative Potential of Political Discussion. *British Journal of Political Science, 32*(1), 21–62. www.cambridge.org/core/journals/british-journal-of-political-science/article/deliberative-potential-of-political-discussion/22C246909942D4AE3B0D21B5826501D9. https://doi.org/10.1017/S0007123402000029.

Converse, P. (1964). The Nature of Belief Systems in Mass Politics. In D. E. Apter (ed.), *Ideology and Discontent*, (pp. 206–261). Ann Arbor: University of Michigan Press.

Crawford, V. P., & Sobel, J. (1982). Strategic Information Transmission. *Econometrica, 50*(6), 1431–1451. www.jstor.org/stable/1913390. https://doi.org/10.2307/1913390.

Crossley, N., Bellotti, E., Edwards, G., Everett, M. G., et al. (2015). *Social Network Analysis for Ego-Nets: Social Network Analysis for Actor-Centred Networks.* London: SAGE.

Dalton, R. J. (2008, March). Citizenship Norms and the Expansion of Political Participation. *Political Studies, 56*(1), 76–98. https://doi.org/10.1111/j.1467-9248.2007.00718.x.

De Dreu, C. K. W., & Boles, T. L. (1998, December). Share and Share Alike or Winner Take All? The Influence of Social Value Orientation upon Choice and Recall of Negotiation Heuristics. *Organizational Behavior and Human Decision Processes, 76*(3), 253–276. www.sciencedirect.com/science/article/pii/S0749597898928060. https://doi.org/10.1006/obhd.1998.2806.

De Dreu, C. K. W., Weingart, L. R., & Kwon, S. (2000). Influence of Social Motives on Integrative Negotiation: A Meta-analytic Review and Test of Two Theories. *Journal of Personality and Social Psychology, 78*(5), 889–905. https://doi.org/10.1037/0022-3514.78.5.889.

Del Ponte, A., Kline, R., & Ryan, J. (2020, May). Behavioral Analysis in the Study of Politics: The Conflict Laboratory. In D. P. Redlawsk (ed.), *The Oxford Encyclopedia of Political Decision Making*. Oxford: Oxford University Press. https://doi.org/10.1093/acrefore/9780190228637.013.1003.

Delli Carpini, M. X., & Keeter, S. (1996). *What Americans Know about Politics and Why It Matters*. New Haven, CT: Yale University Press.

DePaulo, B. M., & Kashy, D. A. (1998). Everyday Lies in Close and Casual Relationships. *Journal of Personality and Social Psychology, 74*(1), 63–79. http://psycnet.apa.org/fulltext/1997-38342-005.html. https://doi.org/10.1037/0022-3514.74.1.63.

Dickson, E. (2011). Economics vs. Psychology Experiments. In J. N. Druckman, D. P. Greene, J. H. Kuklinski & A. Lupia (eds.), *The Handbook of Experimental Political Science* (pp. 58–70). New York: Cambridge University Press. https://nyuseholars.nyu.edu/en/publications/economics-vs-psychology-experiments.

Downs, A. (1957). An Economic Theory of Political Action in a Democracy. *Journal of Political Economy, 65*(2), 135–150.

Druckman, J. N. (2012, June). The Politics of Motivation. *Critical Review, 24*(2), 199–216. https://doi.org/10.1080/08913811.2012.711022.

Druckman, J. N., & Kam, C. D. (2012). Students As Experimental Participants: A Defense of the "Narrow Data Base." In J. N. Druckman, D. P. Green, J. H. Kuklinski, & A. Lupia (eds.), *Handbook of Experimental Political Science* (pp. 41–57). New York: Cambridge University Press.

Druckman, J. N., Klar, S., Krupnikov, Y., Levendusky, M., & Ryan, J. B. (2021, June). (Mis-)Estimating Affective Polarization. *Journal of Politics*, 715603. https://doi.org/10.1086/715603.

Druckman, J. N., & Leeper, T. J. (2012, October). Learning More from Political Communication Experiments: Pretreatment and Its Effects. *American Journal of Political Science, 56*(4), 875–896. https://doi.org/10.1111/j.1540-5907.2012.00582.x.

Druckman, J. N., Levendusky, M. S., & McLain, A. (2018). No Need to Watch: How the Effects of Partisan Media Can Spread via Interpersonal Discussions. *American Journal of Political Science, 62*(1), 99–112. https://doi.org/10.1111/ajps.12325.

Esterling, K. M., Neblo, M. A., & Lazer, D. M. J. (2011, September). Means, Motive, and Opportunity in Becoming Informed about Politics: A Deliberative Field Experiment with Members of Congress and Their Constituents. *Public Opinion Quarterly, 75*(3), 483–503. https://doi.org/10.1093/poq/nfr001.

Eveland, W. P. (2004). The Effect of Political Discussion in Producing Informed Citizens: The Roles of Information, Motivation, and Elaboration. *Political Communication, 21*(2), 177–193. https://doi.org/10.1080/10584600490443877.

Eveland, W. P., Appiah, O., & Beck, P. A. (2017, August). Americans Are More Exposed to Difference than We Think: Capturing Hidden Exposure to Political and Racial Difference. *Social Networks.* www.sciencedirect.com/science/article/pii/S0378873317302113. https://doi.org/10.1016/j.socnet.2017.08.002.

Eveland, W. P., & Kleinman, S. B. (2013, March). Comparing General and Political Discussion Networks within Voluntary Organizations Using Social Network Analysis. *Political Behavior, 35*(1), 65–87. https://doi.org/10.1007/s11109-011-9187-4.

Eveland, W. P., Morey, A. C., & Hutchens, M. J. (2011, December). Beyond Deliberation: New Directions for the Study of Informal Political Conversation from a Communication Perspective. *Journal of Communication, 61*(6), 1082–1103. https://doi.org/10.1111/j.1460-2466.2011.01598.x.

Fehr, E., Goette, L., & Zehnder, C. (2009). A Behavioral Account of the Labor Market: The Role of Fairness Concerns. *Annual Review of Economics, 1*(1), 355–384. https://doi.org/10.1146/annurev.economics.050708.143217.

Fehr, E., & Schmidt, K. M. (1999, August). A Theory of Fairness, Competition, and Cooperation. *Quarterly Journal of Economics, 114*(3), 817–868. https://doi.org/10.1162/003355399556151.

Fishkin, J., Siu, A., Diamond, L., & Bradburn, N. (2021). Is Deliberation an Antidote to Extreme Partisan Polarization? Reflections on "America in One Room." *American Political Science Review.* https://doi.org/10.1017/S0003055421000642.

Fowler, J. H., Heaney, M. T., Nickerson, D. W., Padgett, J. F., & Sinclair, B. (2011, March). Causality in Political Networks. *American Politics Research, 39*(2), 437–480. https://doi.org/10.1177/1532673X10396310.

Gerber, A. S., Huber, G. A., Doherty, D., & Dowling, C. M. (2012, October). Disagreement and the Avoidance of Political Discussion: Aggregate Relationships and Differences across Personality Traits. *American Journal of Political Science, 56*(4), 849–874. https://doi.org/10.1111/j.1540-5907.2011.00571.x.

Grant, A. M. (2007). Relational Job Design and the Motivation to Make a Prosocial Difference. *Academy of Management Review, 32*(2), 393–417. www.jstor.org/stable/20159308. https://doi.org/10.2307/20159308.

Grant, A. M., & Berry, J. W. (2011, February). The Necessity of Others Is The Mother of Invention: Intrinsic and Prosocial Motivations, Perspective Taking, and Creativity. *Academy of Management Journal, 54*(1), 73–96. https://doi.org/10.5465/AMJ.2011.59215085.

Greene, W. H. (2012). *Econometric Analysis* (Seventh ed.). Upper Saddle River, NJ: Prentice Hall.

Groenendyk, E., & Krupnikov, Y. (2021). What Motivates Reasoning? A Theory of Goal-Dependent Political Evaluation. *American Journal of Political Science, 65*(1), 180–196. https://doi.org/10.1111/ajps.12562.

Habermas, J. (1975). *Legitimation Crisis.* Boston, MA: Beacon Press.

Hersh, E. (2020). *Politics Is for Power: How to Move beyond Political Hobbyism, Take Action, and Make Real Change.* New York: Simon and Schuster.

Huckfeldt, R. (1983). Social Contexts, Social Networks, and Urban Neighborhoods: Environmental Constraints on Friendship Choice. *American Journal of Sociology, 89*(3), 651–669.

Huckfeldt, R. (2001). The Social Communication of Political Expertise. *American Journal of Political Science, 45*(2), 425–438.

Huckfeldt, R. (2007, October). Unanimity, Discord, and the Communication of Public Opinion. *American Journal of Political Science, 51*(4), 978–995. https://doi.org/10.1111/j.1540-5907.2007.00292.x.

Huckfeldt, R., Johnson, P. E., & Sprague, J. D. (2004). *Political Disagreement: the Survival of Diverse Opinions within Communication Networks.* New York: Cambridge University Press.

Huckfeldt, R., Levine, J., Morgan, W., & Sprague, J. (1999). Accessibility and the Political Utility of Partisan and Ideological Orientations. *American Journal of Political Science, 43*, 888–911.

Huckfeldt, R., & Mendez, J. M. (2008). Moths, Flames, and Political Engagement: Managing Disagreement within Communication Networks. *Journal of Politics, 70*(01), 83–96. https://doi.org/10.1017/S0022 381607080073.

Huckfeldt, R., Mendez, J. M., & Osborn, T. (2004, February). Disagreement, Ambivalence, and Engagement: The Political Consequences of Heterogeneous Networks. *Political Psychology, 25*(1), 65–95. https://doi.org/10.1111/j.1467-9221.2004.00357.x.

Huckfeldt, R., Pietryka, M. T., & Reilly, J. (2014, January). Noise, Bias, and Expertise in Political Communication networks. *Social Networks, 36*, 110–121. https://doi.org/10.1016/j.socnet.2013.02.003.

Huckfeldt, R., & Sprague, J. (1995). *Citizens, Politics, and Social Communication: Information and Influence in an Election Campaign.* New York: Cambridge University Press.

Jackman, S., & Sniderman, P. M. (2006, May). The Limits of Deliberative Discussion: A Model of Everyday Political Arguments. *Journal of Politics, 68*(2), 272–283. https://doi.org/10.1111/j.1468-2508.2006.00405.x.

Jonas, E., & Frey, D. (2003, July). Information Search and Presentation in Advisor-Client Interactions. *Organizational Behavior and Human Decision Processes, 91*(2), 154–168. www.sciencedirect.com/science/article/pii/S0749597803000591. https://doi.org/10.1016/S0749-5978(03)00059-1.

Jonas, E., Schulz-Hardt, S., & Frey, D. (2005, July). Giving Advice or Making Decisions in Someone Else's Place: The Influence of Impression, Defense, and Accuracy Motivation on the Search for New Information. *Personality and Social Psychology Bulletin, 31*(7), 977–990. http://psp.sagepub.com/content/31/7/977. https://doi.org/10.1177/0146167204274095.

Kam, C. D. (2007, February). When Duty Calls, Do Citizens Answer? *Journal of Politics, 69*(1), 17–29. https://doi.org/10.1111/j.1468-2508.2007.00491.x.

Kamenica, E. (2012). Behavioral Economics and Psychology of Incentives. *Annual Review of Economics, 4*(1), 427–452.

Katz, E. (1957, April). The Two-Step Flow of Communication: An Up-to-Date Report on an Hypothesis. *Public Opinion Quarterly, 21*(1), 61–78. https://doi.org/10.2307/2746790.

Kenny, D. A., & Judd, C.M. (1986). Consequences of Violating the Independence Assumption in Analysis of Variance. *Psychological Bulletin, 99*(3), 422–431. https://doi.org/10.1037/0033-2909.99.3.422.

Kinder, D. R., & Kalmoe, N. P. (2017). *Neither Liberal nor Conservative: Ideological Innocence in the American Public.* Chicago: University of Chicago Press.

Klar, S. (2014, July). Partisanship in a Social Setting. *American Journal of Political Science, 58*(3), 687–704. https://doi.org/10.1111/ajps.12087.

Klar, S., & Krupnikov, Y. (2016). *Independent Politics: How American Disdain for Parties Leads to Political Inaction.* New York: Cambridge University Press.

Klar, S., Krupnikov, Y., & Ryan, J. B. (2018, June). Affective Polarization or Partisan Disdain? Untangling a Dislike for the Opposing Party from a Dislike of Partisanship. *Public Opinion Quarterly, 82*(2), 379–390. https://doi.org/10.1093/poq/nfy014.

Klofstad, C. A., McClurg, S. D., & Rolfe, M. (2009, September). Measurement of Political Discussion Networks: A Comparison of Two "Name Generator" Procedures. *Public Opinion Quarterly, 73*(3), 462–483. https://doi.org/10.1093/poq/nfp032.

Kruglanski, A. W., & Boyatzi, L. M. (2012, June). The Psychology of Closed and Open Mindedness, Rationality, and Democracy. *Critical Review, 24*(2), 217–232. https://doi.org/10.1080/08913811.2012.711023.

Krupnikov, Y., & Levine, A. S. (2014). Cross-Sample Comparisons and External Validity. *Journal of Experimental Political Science, 1*(1), 59–80. www.cambridge.org/core/journals/journal-of-experimental-political-science/article/crosssample-comparisons-and-external-validity/B11437F96788A7F01653A7C1C9E87F34. https://doi.org/10.1017/xps.2014.7.

Krupnikov, Y., & Levine, A. S. (2019, April). Political Issues, Evidence, and Citizen Engagement: The Case of Unequal Access to Affordable Health Care. *Journal of Politics, 81*(2), 385–398. https://doi.org/10.1086/701722.

Krupnikov, Y., Milita, K., Ryan, J. B., & Connors, E. C. (2020, April). How Gender Affects the Efficacy of Discussion As an Information Shortcut. *Political Science Research and Methods, 8*(2), 268–284. www.cambridge.org/core/journals/political-science-research-and-methods/article/abs/how-gender-affects-the-efficacy-of-discussion-as-an-information-shortcut/A1542EAFF4C2D7B71AF0637172FEA954. https://doi.org/10.1017/psrm.2019.26.

Krupnikov, Y., & Ryan, J. B. (2022). *The Other Divide: Polarization and Disengagement in American Politics.* New York: Cambridge University Press.

Kunda, Z. (1990). The Case for Motivated Reasoning. *Psychological Bulletin, 108*(3), 480–498.

Lake, R. L. D., & Huckfeldt, R. (1998). Social Capital, Social Networks, and Political Participation. *Political Psychology, 19*(3), 567–584. https://doi.org/10.1111/0162-895X.00118.

Lau, R. R., & Redlawsk, D. P. (1997, September). Voting Correctly. *American Political Science Review, 91*(3), 585–598. Retrieved 2021-09-03, from www.cambridge.org/core/journals/american-political-science-review/article/abs/voting-correctly/DS6FFS4431588C9BA7675A4A92SA8SSC, https://doi.org/10.2307/2952076.

Lazer, D., Rubineau, B., Chetkovich, C., Katz, N., & Neblo, M. (2010). The Coevolution of Networks and Political Attitudes. *Political Communication, 27*(3), 248–274. https://doi.org/10.1080/10584609.2010.500187.

Leeper, T. J., & Slothuus, R. (2014, February). Political Parties, Motivated Reasoning, and Public Opinion Formation. *Political Psychology, 35*, 129–156. https://doi.org/10.1111/pops.12164.

Lodge, M., & Taber, C. S. (2013). *The Rationalizing Voter.* New York: Cambridge University Press.

Lupia, A., & McCubbins, M. D. (1998). *The Democratic Dilemma: Can Citizens Learn What They Need to Know?* New York: Cambridge University Press.

Lyons, J., & Sokhey, A. (2014, April). Emotion, Motivation, and Social Information Seeking about Politics. *Political Communication, 31*(2), 237–258. http://dx.doi.org/10.1080/10584609.2013.828138.

Makse, T., Minkoff, S., & Sokhey, A. (2019). *Politics on Display: Yard Signs and the Politicization of Social Spaces.* Oxford University Press.

Makse, T., Minkoff, S. L., & Sokhey, A. E. (2014, September). Networks, Context, and the Use of Spatially Weighted Survey Metrics. *Political Geography, 42*, 79–91. www.sciencedirect.com/science/article/pii/S0962629814000596. https://doi.org/10.1016/j.polgeo.2014.07.003.

Maxwell, S. E., Delaney, H. D., & Kelley, K. (2017). *Designing Experiments and Analyzing Data: A Model Comparison Perspective, Third Edition.* New York: Routledge.

McClurg, S. D. (2006, July). The Electoral Relevance of Political Talk: Examining Disagreement and Expertise Effects in Social Networks on Political Participation. *American Journal of Political Science, 50*(3), 737–754. https://doi.org/10.1111/j.1540-5907.2006.00213.x.

Mendelberg, T. (2002). The Deliberative Citizen: Theory and Evidence. In M. X. Delli Carpini, L. Huddy, & R. Shapiro (eds.), *Political Decision Making, Deliberation and Participation* (Vol. 6, pp. 151–193). Greenwich, CT: JAI Press.

Miller, J. M., Saunders, K. L., & Farhart, C. E. (2016, October). Conspiracy Endorsement As Motivated Reasoning: The Moderating Roles of Political Knowledge and Trust. *American Journal of Political Science, 60*(4), 824–844. https://doi.org/10.1111/ajps.12234.

Minozzi, W., Song, H., Lazer, D. M. J., Neblo, M. A., & Ognyanova, K. (2020). The Incidental Pundit: Who Talks Politics with Whom, and Why? *American Journal of Political Science, 64*(1), 135–151. https://doi.org/10.1111/ajps.12469.

Montgomery, J. M., Nyhan, B., & Torres, M. (2018, July). How Conditioning on Posttreatment Variables Can Ruin Your Experiment and What to Do about It. *American Journal of Political Science, 62*(3), 760–775. https://doi.org/10.1111/ajps.12357.

Mullinix, K. J. (2018, March). Civic Duty and Political Preference Formation. *Political Research Quarterly, 71*(1), 199–214. https://doi.org/10.1177/1065912917729037.

Mutz, D. C. (2006). *Hearing the Other Side: Deliberative versus Participatory Democracy.* New York: Cambridge University Press.

Mutz, D. C., & Mondak, J. J. (2006, February). The Workplace As a Context for Cross-Cutting Political Discourse. *Journal of Politics, 68*(1), 140–155. https://doi.org/10.1111/j.1468-2508.2006.00376.x.

Neblo, M. A. (2015). *Deliberative Democracy between Theory and Practice.* New York: Cambridge University Press.

Petersen, M. B., Skov, M., Serritzlew, S., & Ramsoy, T. (2013). Motivated Reasoning and Political Parties: Evidence for Increased Processing in the Face of Party Cues. *Political Behavior, 35*(4), 831–854. https://doi.org/10.1007/s11109-012-9213-1.

Pietryka, M. T. (2016, June). Accuracy Motivations, Predispositions, and Social Information in Political Discussion Networks. *Political Psychology, 37*(3), 367–386. https://doi.org/10.1111/pops.12255.

Pietryka, M. T., Reilly, J. L., Maliniak, D. M., Miller, P. R., Huckfeldt, R., & Rapoport, R. B. (2018). From Respondents to Networks: Bridging Between Individuals, Discussants, and the Network in the Study of Political Discussion. *Political Behavior, 40*(3), 711–735. https://doi.org/10.1007/s11109-017-9419-3.

Preston, S. D., & Waal, F. B. M. D. (2002, February). Empathy: Its Ultimate and Proximate Bases. *Behavioral and Brain Sciences, 25*(1), 1–20. www.cambridge.org/core/journals/behavioral-and-brain-sciences/article/empathy-its-ultimate-and-proximate-bases/953ESDS92176FEE351ED81E933FE646D. https://doi.org/10.1017/S0140525X02000018.

Prior, M. (2005). News vs. Entertainment: How Increasing Media Choice Widens Gaps in Political Knowledge and Turnout. *American Journal of Political Science, 49*(3), 577–592 http://onlinelibrary.wiley.com/doi/10.1111/j.1540--5907.2005.00143.x/abstract.

Putnam, R. P. (2000). *Bowling Alone.* New York: Simon & Schuster.

Robison, J., Stevenson, R. T., Druckman, J. N., Jackman, S., Katz, J. N., & Vavreck, L. (2018, July). An Audit of Political Behavior Research. *SAGE Open, 8*(3), 2158244018794769. https://doi.org/10.1177/2158244018794769.

Roese, N. J., & Vohs, K. D. (2012, September). Hindsight Bias. *Perspectives on Psychological Science, 7*(5), 411–426. https://doi.org/10.1177/1745691612454303.

Rolfe, M. (2012). *Voter Turnout: A Social Theory of Political Participation.* New York: Cambridge University Press.

Ryan, J. B. (2010). The Effects of Network Expertise and Biases on Vote Choice. *Political Communication, 27*(1), 44–58. https://doi.org/10.1080/10584600903481893.

Ryan, J. B. (2011a, June). Accuracy and Bias in Perceptions of Political Knowledge. *Political Behavior, 33*(2), 335–356. https://doi.org/10.1007/s11109-010-9130-0.

Ryan, J. B. (2011b, October). Social Networks As a Shortcut to Correct Voting. *American Journal of Political Science, 55*(4), 753–766. https://doi.org/10.1111/j.1540-5907.2011.00528.x.

Sanders, L. M. (1997). Against Deliberation. *Political Theory, 25*(3), 347–376. www.jstor.org/stable/191984.

Sears, D. O. (1986). College Sophomores in the Laboratory: Influences of a Narrow Data Base on Social Psychology's View of Human Nature. *Journal of Personality and Social Psychology, 51*(3), 515–530. https://doi.org/10.1037/0022-3514.51.3.515.

Settle, J. E. (2018). *Frenemies: How Social Media Polarizes America.* New York: Cambridge University Press.

Settle, J. E., & Carlson, T. N. (2019, July). Opting Out of Political Discussions. *Political Communication, 36*(3), 476–496. https://doi.org/10.1080/10584609.2018.1561563.

Shepsle, K. A. (1972, June). The Strategy of Ambiguity: Uncertainty and Electoral Competition. *American Political Science Review, 66*(2), 555–568. www.jstor.org/stable/1957799. https://doi.org/10.2307/1957799.

Siegel, D. A. (2009, January). Social Networks and Collective Action. *American Journal of Political Science, 53*(1), 122–138. https://doi.org/10.1111/j.1540-5907.2008.00361.x.

Sinclair, B., McConnell, M., & Green, D. P. (2012, October). Detecting Spillover Effects: Design and Analysis of Multilevel Experiments. *American Journal of Political Science, 56*(4), 1055–1069. https://doi.org/10.1111/j.1540-5907.2012.00592.x.

Smith, V. L. (1982). Microeconomic Systems As an Experimental Science. *American Economic Review, 72*(5), 923–955. www.jstor.org/stable/1812014.

Snijders, T. A. B., & Roel J. Bosker. (2012). *Multilevel Analysis: An Introduction to Basic and Advanced Multilevel Modeling* (Second ed.). London: SAGE.

Sokhey, A. E., & McClurg, S. D. (2012, July). Social Networks and Correct Voting. *Journal of Politics, 74*(03), 751–764. https://doi.org/10.1017/S0022381612000461.

Song, H., & Eveland, W. P. (2015, January). The Structure of Communication Networks Matters: How Network Diversity, Centrality, and Context Influence Political Ambivalence, Participation, and Knowledge. *Political Communication, 32*(1), 83–108. https://doi.org/10.1080/10584609.2014.882462.

Taber, C. S., & Lodge, M. (2006). Motivated Skepticism in the Evaluation of Political Beliefs. *American Journal of Political Science, 50*(3), 755–769.

Tappin, B. M., Pennycook, G., & Rand, D. G. (2020). Rethinking the Link between Cognitive Sophistication and Politically Motivated Reasoning. *Journal of Experimental Psychology: General.* https://doi.org/10.1037/xge0000974.

Tetlock, P. E. (1985). Accountability: The Neglected Social Context of Judgment and Choice. *Research in Organizational Behavior, 7*(1), 297–332.

Tetlock, P. E., & Kim, J. I. (1987, April). Accountability and Judgment Processes in a Personality Prediction Task. *Journal of Personality and Social Psychology, 52*(4), 700–709.

Walsh, K. C. (2004). *Talking about Politics: Informal Groups and Social Identity in American Life.* Chicago: University of Chicago Press.

Ward, M. D., & Gleditsch, K. S. (2008). *Spatial Regression Models* (First ed.). Thousand Oaks, CA: SAGE.

Warren, M. (1992, March). Democratic Theory and Self-Transformation. *American Political Science Review, 86*(01), 8–23. https://doi.org/10.2307/1964012.

Weingart, L. R., Bennett, R. J., & Brett, J. M. (1993). The Impact of Consideration of Issues and Motivational Orientation on Group Negotiation Process and Outcome. *Journal of Applied Psychology, 78*(3), 504–517. http://psycnet.apa.org/journals/apl/78/3/504.html. https://doi.org/10.1037/0021-9010.78.3.504.

Zaller, J. R. (1992). *The Nature and Origins of Mass Opinion.* New York: Cambridge University Press.

Acknowledgments

We are grateful for the helpful comments we have received about this project from Bob Huckfeldt, Elias Assaf, Quintin Beazer, Bill Berry, Robert Bond, Cheryl Boudreau, Taylor Carlson, Brad Gomez, Michael Neblo, Kai Ou, Judd Thornton, Steven Webster, Jamie Druckman, and two anonymous reviewers. We also thank Kelley Doll, Dennis Langley, and Jessica Parsons for assistance conducting the experiments. Last, we thank our family members, both human and fur, two of whom attempted to snuggle their way into coauthorship but eventually took too many naps to achieve this status.

Cambridge Elements ≡

Experimental Political Science

James N. Druckman

Northwestern University

James N. Druckman is the Payson S. Wild Professor of Political Science and the Associate Director of the Institute for Policy Research at Northwestern University. He served as an editor for the journals Political Psychology and Public Opinion Quarterly as well as the University of Chicago Press's series in American Politics. He currently is the co-Principal Investigator of Time-Sharing Experiments for the Social Sciences (TESS) and sits on the American National Election Studies' Board. He previously served as President of the American Political Science Association section on Experimental Research and helped oversee the launching of the Journal of Experimental Political Science. He was co-editor of the Cambridge Handbook of Experimental Political Science. He is a Fellow of the American Academy of Arts and Sciences and has published more than 100 articles/book chapters on public opinion, political communication, campaigns, research methods, and other topics.

About the Series

There currently are few outlets for extended works on experimental methodology in political science. The new Experimental Political Science Cambridge Elements series features research on experimental approaches to a given substantive topic, and experimental methods by prominent and upcoming experts in the field.

Cambridge Elements ᵔ

Experimental Political Science

Elements in the Series